Louise Heren is a television producer and director with established credentials in childcare observational documentaries. Susan McMillan is an award-winning television producer and writer. She lectures in creative writing and has written for BBC Books as well as numerous television scripts. Together they have written, filmed and produced many documentaries, including *Special Babies* and *Nanny School*, which involved them spending a year at Norland College. They have written this book in association with the childcare experts at Norland College.

nanny
in a book

THE COMMON-SENSE GUIDE TO CHILDCARE

LOUISE HEREN AND
SUSAN MCMILLAN

1 3 5 7 9 10 8 6 4 2

Published in 2011 by Vermilion, an imprint of Ebury Publishing

Ebury Publishing is a Random House Group company

Copyright © Louise Heren and Susan McMillan 2011
Copyright illustrations © Stephen Dew 2011

The Random House Group Limited Reg. No. 954009

Addresses for companies within the Random House Group can be found at
www.randomhouse.co.uk

A CIP catalogue record for this book is available from the British Library

The Random House Group Limited supports The Forest Stewardship
Council (FSC), the leading international forest certification organisation.
All our titles that are printed on Greenpeace approved FSC certified paper
carry the FSC logo. Our paper procurement policy can be found at
www.randomhouse.co.uk

Mixed Sources

Product group from well-managed
forests and other controlled sources
www.fsc.org Cert no. TT-COC-2139
© 1996 Forest Stewardship Council

Designed and set by seagulls.net

Printed and bound in Great Britain by CPI Mackays, Chatham, ME5 8TD

ISBN 9780091935467

Copies are available at special rates for bulk orders.
Contact the sales development team on 020 7840 8487 for more information.

To buy books by your favourite authors and register for offers,
visit www.randomhouse.co.uk

The information in this book has been compiled by way of general guidance in relation
to the specific subjects addressed, but is not a substitute and not to be relied on for
medical, healthcare, pharmaceutical or other professional advice on specific circumstances
and in specific locations. Please consult your GP before changing, stopping or starting
any medical treatment. So far as the authors are aware the information given is correct
and up to date as at October 2010. Practice, laws and regulations all change, and the
reader should obtain up to date professional advice on any such issues. The authors and
publishers disclaim, as far as the law allows, any liability arising directly or indirectly
from the use, or misuse, of the information contained in this book.

CONTENTS

why every parent needs this book

When we were expecting our babies, we wanted a practical handbook that took a common-sense approach to raising a family and put the fun back into childhood. We did not want a 'one size fits all' approach or personal stories from celebrity mums; we wanted advice based on years of hands-on experience. There was clearly a gap on the childcare bookshelves.

It was when we were asked to make a television series about the world-renowned Norland Nannies that we realised their approach was what we had been missing. There is a reason why royalty and celebrities employ Norland Nannies – they are the best. If only we could have afforded a Norland Nanny ... Then it occurred to us. We could have a Norland Nanny in spirit – in a book.

Like many modern mothers, we had forgotten many of the childcare methods that our grandmothers knew worked. The advice in this book therefore combines 21st-century childcare practice with the traditional 'no-nonsense' approach – a formula that has worked for generations of grannies and nannies.

This book will help you to recapture the simple approach to parenting. We have written it for families who are looking for common-sense advice with no time for nonsense.

Louise Heren and Susan McMillan

NB: We've used the terms 'he', 'him' and 'his' for all babies, male and female. We're not being sexist; it's just made writing this book much easier.

INTRODUCTION
nanny knows best

The English nanny is an institution. The image of the smartly uniformed traditional nanny is perpetuated by books and films, and there is something rather comforting about the idea of a 'no-nonsense', nurturing and sensible childcare expert looking after your family. She will ensure that your children are healthy, happy and thoroughly well brought-up. The Norland Nanny is all of this and more; she is a Mary Poppins for the 21st century.

For over a century, Norland Nannies have cared for royal and celebrity families. Their reputation is based on the experience of generations of English nannies and has been tried and tested on thousands of families. Now you do not have to be a Hollywood actress or a duchess to have a Norland Nanny for your own family. *Nanny in a Book* is a practical companion to childhood, from day one to age eight, packed full of Nanny's top tips and personal anecdotes.

The experts at Norland College in Bath are at the forefront of the latest thinking on childcare and child development, and they train the best and most respected nannies in the world. So unlike other childcare books, this one is based on a century of *experience*, not on personal opinion. These nannies have 'road tested' more children than all other childcare gurus put together. Whether it is getting children to sleep, organising a fabulous birthday party or globetrotting with toddlers, when it comes to putting your child first Nanny definitely knows best.

CHAPTER 1
nanny in the nursery

Over the years, Norland Nannies have cared for thousands of newborn babies, all as individual as your baby. So if anyone can give advice on those first few weeks of motherhood, Nanny can.

In this chapter, Nanny will give you expert information on how to set up your nursery and choose the best baby equipment. There will also be top tips on feeding, nappy changing and bathing – in fact, everything you will need to help you and your baby through the early months together.

Setting up a Nursery

If you are short of time, there are a few essentials that can be assembled in a matter of hours; the fancier baby equipment can be sourced at a later stage. The absolute essentials for coping in those first hours home are:

- 3 babygros
- 1 pack of nappies (it helps to get the right size; the packets have a guide on the side)
- An old towel to use as a changing mat
- A shawl or blanket to wrap the baby in

Armed with these items, you can change your baby's clothes and bottom, and keep him warm. They will keep you going for a couple of days until help arrives or you feel like venturing out.

However, assuming you have not gone into labour in the supermarket, this is how Nanny gets a nursery ready for its new inhabitant.

DECORATING

It is easy to get carried away with lots of colour and friezes of tractors or fairies, but remember your baby cannot focus properly for the first few weeks of his life, so try to keep colours neutral and do not make the walls busy with too many pictures. This also means that whatever sex your baby is, you will not be stereotyping him or her with blue or pink, or trains and dolls, from the start. Yellows and creams are good and rarely go out of fashion; they are also calming and restful. You and your baby will be spending a lot of time together in this room; anything too garish could become irritating for you.

In his very first weeks, your baby sees the world in black and white. Bold blocks of these two colours will help his brand new eyes to focus and will develop his interest in the world. After the first month, shapes and things that sparkle and shine will be important to your baby. It is worth thinking about putting coloured shapes on the wall or simple pictures that will catch his eye. He will spend quite a lot of time looking at the ceiling while being changed, so do not rule it out as a potential canvas for shiny pictures or mobiles.

NURSERY FURNITURE

It is not essential to kit out your baby's new room with the latest furniture, but a few items will make his and your life easier in the first months.

Cot

This is your baby's bed and somewhere for him to feel safe. For the first six months, it is recommended that your baby sleeps in your room with you. This makes night-time feeding easier and means you can check your baby as many times as you like during the night. Nanny always looks for a cot with:

- bars on all four sides for ventilation and so your baby can see through
- one side that slides down or collapses in some way to enable you to lift your baby out without straining your back
- a locking system for the collapsible side – this will be very handy when your baby is able to stand in his cot and rattle the sides
- sides high enough to contain an 18-month to 2-year-old who is standing up (approximately 1 metre)
- a firm, breathable and new mattress – this is one item to spend a little bit more money on if you can

If you do nothing else before having your baby, do assemble the cot.

Moses Basket

If a full-sized cot does not fit into your bedroom, a Moses basket is an option, although this might be an expense too far. Often a carrycot that transfers to a set of pram wheels to become a full pram is a more flexible option, but if you like the look of Moses baskets, there are some things you should consider:

- Never pick the basket up by the handles with the baby in it. The handles are rarely strong enough even for the lightest baby.
- Look for a basket with soft weaving material. Anything with sharp edges or fraying pieces is unsuitable.
- A loose weave is best for ventilation.

- If the basket is second-hand, do buy a new mattress for it.
- A washable lining is essential.

Carrycot

A carrycot is a sturdy portable cot that looks similar to the top part of a baby's traditional pram. It can double up as a daytime cot for downstairs and will also attach to a set of wheels for outings. Although carrycots may not come in the latest bright colours with the side bags and straps you find on more modern car seat-to-pram combinations, they are very practical and have stood the test of time.

Cot Bedding

Sheets and blankets for the cot should be made from natural fibres. You will be well prepared with a pack of three fitted cotton sheets for the mattress, a mattress protector, three flat sheets for on top and three cotton or wool-mix blankets. These can be used in the cot or basket, and should be enough for you not to have to do laundry every day.

Baby blankets come in all colours and sizes. The basics you are looking for are a combination of cotton and wool to cope with varying temperatures throughout the day. Old-fashioned wool-mix cell blankets with bound edges – the ones with the square holes in them – are still Nanny's firm favourite. They wear well and wash and dry quickly, and prevent your baby from getting too hot.

A baby under one year old should never have a pillow, quilt or duvet. He can wriggle under them without being able to wriggle back out, and can therefore get into difficulties. See 'Sleep' (page 37) for more advice on how to put your baby to bed correctly.

Cot bumpers are not recommended for babies under one year. They hinder good ventilation around the cot, and a baby who can almost stand may use a cot bumper to pull himself up, becoming tangled in the process. They have lovely designs, but it is best to wait if you are going to use them. Later, when your baby is more agile, cot bumpers can stop flailing arms getting caught in cot bars, or an active sleeper from bumping his head on the sides.

Changing Unit

As your baby drifts off to sleep in his new cot, you may realise that he has a wet or dirty nappy. Since no one wants to wake a sleeping baby, it is best to get into the habit of changing him before every sleep, and for that you will need somewhere safe and clean.

After more than a century of changing thousands of babies, Nanny still advocates an old towel or changing mat on the floor as the best way to change a baby EVER. You can reach all the creams, nappies and clean clothes you need, and can place them out of baby's reach on the floor; and if there is an emergency, you can respond knowing that your baby is safe and cannot roll off a table or other surface. However, there are a lot of tempting baby changing units on the market. The best ones are designed with both you *and* the baby in mind, so you are looking for a unit that has:

- enough room for the baby to lie on and wave his arms around and kick his legs (remember he is going to grow and you may still be changing nappies after his second birthday)
- sufficient room for you to lay out a nappy and a pot of cream
- baskets or drawers underneath that open easily and are within arm's reach
- a peg or hook on the end for a nappy sack – you could always attach a hook of your own if necessary

There is only one strict rule Nanny applies to babies on baby changing units or tabletops of any kind – **always keep one hand on the baby**. Never leave a baby unrestrained on a tabletop.

Nursing Chair

A clean, warm and replete baby will sleep well, so feeding him before you put him down is very good practice. Having a place for you and your baby to sit comfortably and quietly for as long as it takes will work wonders for your stress levels, and his. It is the start of a routine that will program your baby into nodding off.

Nanny uses a nursing chair or moves a favourite comfy chair into the nursery. Some nursing chairs rock, but getting your baby accustomed to motion to feed or go to sleep may cause issues when you want him to sleep and the nursing chair or pram are not available. Just an ordinary comfortable chair that you like is good enough.

Always remove your outdoor shoes before entering the nursery. Your baby will spend a lot of time lying on the floor or crawling around his bedroom and you can bet he will find the tiniest speck of dirt and put it into his mouth. Once your baby has learned to grasp things, he will tug at the corners of rugs. Consider a fitted carpet for the nursery or a rug that can be held down by furniture.

NANNY'S TOP TIP

Slip-on shoes just as easily slip off – wear lace-ups or buckled shoes while carrying your baby. They will not slip off at that crucial moment and trip you up. It may sound old fashioned, but this is one of Nanny's sensible rules.

Nightlight

Although a nightlight is not necessary for helping your baby go off to sleep, a low lamp you can switch on when checking on him that does not create a blaze of light could be useful.

OTHER BABY PARAPHERNALIA

The modern baby has a long shopping list of 'essentials'. You can buy all or some of the items in the following list. Choose items that suit your budget and the way you want to care for your baby:

- Car seat (see below)
- Pram (see page 8)
- Sling or pouch (see page 10)
- Backpack (see page 11)
- Baby monitor (see page 11)
- Baby room thermometer (see page 11)
- Baby clothes (see page 12)
- Baby toys (see page 13)

Car Seat

A car seat is essential these days. If you are going home from hospital by car or taxi, you will not be allowed to leave without a suitable car seat. In fact, most hospitals will inspect your car seat for worthiness before placing your baby in it and carrying it to the hospital exit for you. Hospital staff are responsible for the care of your newborn while you are on hospital premises. However, they do not have the space to store car seats, so try not to turn up in labour fully prepared with a car seat tucked under your arm; arrange for someone to bring it in for you when you are certain you are going home. If you do not think you will need a car seat once home, borrow one from a trusted source for that first journey into the wide world.

The car seat should support your baby fully and his head should not poke out above the headrest. It should have two straps – one over each shoulder – and the buckle should fasten tightly in the middle and be adjustable as your baby grows. The baby seat should have anchor points to fix it to your rear passenger seat. If you have time before the birth, it is worth practising fitting the car seat at home. It can take a long time for beginners to get this right and the midwife may be standing on the kerbside waiting to wave you off!

A baby's car seat should never be put in a passenger seat with an airbag. These can kill babies and smaller children if they go off so put your baby in the back seat in the rear-facing position. He should be in a rear-facing car seat for as long as possible. This position gives better head and neck support to your baby should you be in a crash. Check the weight limit for your car seat and keep your baby in his rear-facing seat for as long as the weight limit permits, and at least until your baby can sit up unaided.

Pram

Prams get Norland Nannies very excited, particularly those robust coachwork-built prams. These fine prams will certainly make you stand out in a crowd of proud parents. They are Nanny's traditional choice because they are high up and keep your baby away from car exhaust fumes; they allow the baby and the adult to make eye contact, thus encouraging communication; they are stable and sturdy, and will last for generations.

However, they are not light. Today, it is probably best to use them for walks rather than trying to manoeuvre them round shopping centres. So if you are looking for something modern, test a few prams before buying.

A pram designed with you in mind allows you to face your baby. You can talk to him and smile, and he can see you pointing at interesting things. Your pram should also have good brakes, be easy to steer and have a shopping basket underneath or side bags balanced on both sides. It should be stable but not too heavy. A hand strap is useful to wrap around your wrist so that if for any reason you and the pram handle become detached, the pram cannot become a runaway vehicle.

A pram designed with your baby in mind allows him to face you so that he can communicate with you by smiling and gesturing, and later you can talk to one another. There is good research that shows that a parent-facing pram develops your child's communication skills, which can only help him succeed later in life. Nanny also likes to see prams with anchor points for a harness or reins to ensure your baby cannot wriggle out or be tipped out. It should be padded all round with no sharp or pointed parts. The baby must have sufficient room to lie flat to keep his spine straight and supported. A rain cover and sun shield are also necessary. For a cheap alternative to a parasol, clip a muslin square to the hood with two clothes pegs.

Baby Travel Systems

There are many baby travel systems on the market, and these might work for you, but there is a risk. The baby often spends his day in the car seat part of a travel system. He lies in it in the car. He is carried into a house or pushed to a café in the travel system, and he is left in it during his visit. He falls asleep there and is put back into the car to go home; and while his mum is getting his milk ready, the car seat with him in it is balanced on a kitchen work surface. If a multi-purpose baby travel system is your way forward, remember your new baby needs to lie flat for most of the day. He will grow up with a straight healthy spine and may even be an early walker for it. The recommended time limit for your baby to stay in his car seat is two hours, but far less is preferable.

As with all baby equipment, test your pram or baby travel system before using it. Practise collapsing it, preferably with one hand (the other will probably have your baby in it when you need to do this for real) and see if you can lift it into the boot of your car.

Nanny always uses a pram for a tiny baby. A pushchair or stroller does not give sufficient support to your baby's spine and head. It is worth waiting six months or more before you purchase a pushchair; you can often sell your pram at a children's second-hand or nearly new store and buy a buggy when the time is right. Babies can get rather expensive to maintain, so do check out second-hand options.

Sling or Pouch

Pouches and slings are not just for shopping trips. They are really useful for keeping your baby close while you get on with jobs around the house and garden. Your baby will want to nestle up facing you at first, but after a few months, he will want to turn round and see the world he lives in. A simple sarong that is long and strong enough will do, but there are some more technical slings and pouches on the market today that are safer. Have a look around and try a few out for comfort.

You are looking for a pouch that has a padded shoulder strap over both your shoulders. It will have some form of waist and back support, and strong clasps for keeping the harness in place. The pouch the baby sits in will be padded, soft and warm with large enough holes for arms and legs eventually to poke out. Check the weight limits on the pouch or sling before you buy as some will take a heavier baby than others. If your baby starts life with a higher birth weight, then it may not be long before he outgrows his pouch if he continues to grow quickly. Slings should have all these elements and be long enough to give you support over both shoulders and round your waist.

NANNY'S TOP TIP

If you have twins, but cannot manoeuvre a twins' pram, then take one baby in the pram and one in a sling. Remember to alternate them for each trip out.

Backpack

A backpack can be used once your baby is able to sit up and keep his head upright unaided. Although not an essential item, it is very useful for the active family. Look for one that fits your back but will adjust to fit your partner, and one that is suitably sized for your baby with sufficient growing room. Some backpacks have detachable rain hoods and sun shields, and it is useful to find one that has a few pockets to accommodate essential bottles, beakers, a spare nappy and a hat, and a clip for your house keys.

Baby Monitor

These come with two parts – one for your baby's room and one for you. They are usually mains powered although some also run on batteries. Monitors are not essential for newborns because your baby should be sleeping day and night in the same room as you until he is six months old. Once he is beyond this stage, and you can put your baby down in his cot during the day while you get on with some jobs in another room, a baby monitor becomes essential. You can listen in without constantly running in and out, but do pop in every 15 minutes for a visual check on him. There are also baby video monitors on the market so that you can see him asleep as well as hear him.

There is only one tiny problem with any baby monitor. Remember to keep your voice low if you go to check your baby because you never know who is listening at the other end.

Baby Room Thermometer

This is an essential item. Your baby's room should be well ventilated but not draughty, and not too hot or cold. A temperature of around 18°–20°C is ideal. A room thermometer will help you keep the room's temperature just right.

Baby Clothes

Although baby clothes are irresistible to any new family, there are certain things you should look out for before you go on a spending spree. The newborn's clothes should be made from 100 per cent natural fibres. Choose cotton, keeping wool for top layers so it is not directly next to your baby's skin. Baby clothes should not have pieces that could be pulled off and put in the mouth. Anything too fluffy or furry, particularly round the neck or face, could cause irritation.

Your new baby will grow rapidly so do not buy stacks of babygros in newborn size because he will probably have grown out of them within the first month. Babygros in size 0–3 months will probably suit a larger newborn and will get most babies through those early weeks before you have to go shopping again. Being too thrifty at this stage and buying clothes in size 3–6 months might mean that your baby is not comfortable or warm enough.

As to colour, well Nanny recommends plain and simple. If you do not know if you are having a boy or girl, just a few white babygros will make your baby look simply adorable. Having a few things in stock before your baby arrives is helpful. Once home, you may be lucky enough to be given baby clothes as presents. As your baby gets bigger, you may find he is getting through several outfits every day if he is a very messy baby.

Nanny's Layette Checklist:
- 3 babygros
- 3 under vests (for a winter baby)
- 2 pairs of mittens
- 2 pull-on hats
- Shawl or blanket
- All-in-one snowsuit or fleece bodysuit for trips out
- 6 cotton muslin squares

NANNY'S TOP TIP

Tiny fingers and toes bend backwards easily when getting dressed, so when putting on sleeves and leggings, scrunch up the material like you would when putting on a sock. Put your fingertips through the wrist or ankle hole, and gently clasp his fist or foot and pull it through. This way his fingers or toes are not lost in the length of material and you can pull the sleeve up his arm without injury.

Baby shoes and booties are a luxury for your newborn and unnecessary. As long as his feet are warm, then he will be happy, and you can achieve that simply by wrapping his blanket round them. If you do buy booties, ensure they are big enough for his feet with some growing room. Likewise, socks should be big enough to allow toes to wriggle. Ill-fitting socks are just as damaging to soft feet as poorly fitted shoes.

Baby Toys

Although baby toys are very tempting, for the first six weeks or so, you are your baby's best toy. Everything he sees, smells and hears is generated from his immediate surroundings. His first lessons in life will come from his family. Most babies' first toy is a cuddly soft teddy. They are always a favourite but are not recommended for newborns, so do not put them in your baby's cot or pram. Soft toys are not advised for your child until he is at least a year old. Fluff can irritate him or become a choking hazard; being too close to a teddy could overheat him, and a floppy teddy could fall on him in his cot and smother him.

These days, all manufactured toys have a safety standards label that will also give you an age and stage range. Do check this for everything you buy or are given. No one will be offended if you pop something away in the toy basket for a month or even longer. If you are buying a cuddly toy for your baby to enjoy later, then make sure it is not too furry; check the eyes to ensure they are stitched in and not buttons or beads, and do not be tempted by anything too big – it could be overwhelming to a younger baby.

MAKING A PRAM WINDMILL

Pram toys are easily lost in the bustle of shopping, so here is one that you can make at home for little cost and replace when it flies away.

Take a square of stiff coloured card and cut it into triangles the way you would a sandwich. Insert a flat-headed drawing pin through the inside or middle point of each triangle to pin them together with a central spindle. Then take the right-hand outer corner, fold it into the centre and fix it on to the pin. Do this with all four triangles.

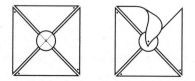

You can mount the sails on a gardener's stick or a straw, and push the free end into a cork for safety. Now you can attach it to the pram and watch your baby's delight seeing it blow round as you go for a walk.

Smaller soft toys that he can pick up and hold in a couple of months' time are probably more suitable as first toys, but should never be left in the cot or pram with him unsupervised by you.

Rattles, soft building blocks and rag books are all good toys for your baby's first learning experiences. Keep toys soft, colourful and interesting in the first months and, above all, washable. Once your baby can hold up his head or is rolling or sitting aided by cushions, then toys become necessary for him to develop basic skills like grasping and hand–eye coordination. He will shake his toys and chew them, figuring out what the world tastes like and how it feels.

One toy Nanny does not approve of is the musical baby gym with flashing lights. Babies, like their parents, will become agitated and irritable if the noise and flashing lights continue incessantly so close to their faces. Your baby cannot reach up and switch it off when it becomes annoying, so if you do have one of these toys, remember to switch it off. Ten minutes is the limit.

I modified my plastic baby gym once my charges were older. I removed all the hanging toys and replaced them with securely fastened natural objects; things like dried seedless pine cones and clean large feathers. **Nanny Julia**

Now you have brought your baby home, assembled all his accessories and are getting to know one another, it is time to plan your days.

Settling in with Your New Baby

Nanny knows that a new baby changes your life forever. Like any new relationship, it takes time to get to know one another. With every new baby Nanny cares for, the first thing she does is observe him. For instance, she will find out whether he likes being touched a lot or a little, how he likes to be held and how much milk he will take at a single feed – all these things need to be learned gradually. So like any Norland Nanny, watch and listen. He will quickly let you know if he likes his feet gently massaged or if you are burping him the most successful way.

Remember that your baby's care is centred around him. Establish a routine in the early days but keep clear of setting yourselves a timetable. Nanny's message is enjoy yourselves, learn together and, when necessary, let your baby lead you. He will let you know what works for him, and therefore what will make your life easier too.

Here are the things you will find yourself fitting into your new routine.

MILK FEEDING

Feeding your baby is going to take up a lot of your day. A newborn will need feeds every two to four hours. How much he needs and how long he takes to swallow each feed will be down to him. Any medical professional will tell you breast is best and Nanny agrees, but Nanny will never pass comment on whatever you choose because you have made your decision for your own reasons.

If you are breastfeeding, ask your midwife lots of questions before you leave hospital. A practical demonstration from her with you and your baby beats a book description. She will be able to show you how your baby will latch on, and how to hold him and your breast to give him access. You can keep asking questions when you get home. Your health visitor, mum or friend might have some useful tips that work for you and your baby. If you are having difficulties, try everything that is suggested. Know when it is not working and move on to the next idea; eventually you will both learn how to do it. If it does not work out, then there are always bottles to try.

Whether you are breast- or bottle-feeding, the first step is to **wash your hands**. A newborn is particularly susceptible to infection so give him a fighting chance of staying well by not introducing any germs into his milk.

Every new mum should do her best to remain healthy and rested but breastfeeding can be particularly exhausting, especially if you have twins or a hungry baby. Ensure you get enough to eat and keep yourself hydrated – sipping from a cold drink beside your nursing chair every time you sit down to feed will mean you are getting enough to drink (avoid hot drinks that can scald if dropped). If you need to take any medicines, check with your doctor that they are suitable while breastfeeding. Avoid caffeine and alcohol, and do not smoke. There is caffeine in cocoa so, sadly, go steady on the chocolate too.

When to Feed
There are two methods – feeding on demand and feeding on schedule. The first is time consuming, but your baby will put on weight faster and it may help you establish breastfeeding more quickly. This might be easier for experienced mums. Feeding on schedule might suit a first-time mum better. Feed every two to four hours, but do not just rely on the clock – remember to check for signs of hunger frequently. Only you will know what signals your newborn gives off when he is hungry, so learn to observe him in the first days and tune into him. Feeding on schedule also means you can plan your day around feeds as long as there is some flexibility for your baby to have an opinion too.

Where to Feed
Get yourself comfortable in your chosen nursing chair before you start. Your baby may be a slow feeder and you could be sitting

here for some time. Feeding by breast or bottle is not to be rushed, and is time for you to concentrate all your attention on your baby.

Feeding twins takes more time and space. A lot of mums find it hard to decide which twin to feed first. If you can, remove that difficult decision by feeding them simultaneously, one to each breast supported by a pillow and your hands holding their heads. You will be more tired feeding two, so try harder to eat well and drink lots of fluids. Your babies will thank you for it – one day!

NANNY'S TOP TIP

Do not wear perfume while your baby is tiny. He needs to learn your smell, and he may also find perfume an irritant to his nose or skin.

Breast or Bottle?

Some mums decide to move on from breast to bottle at a later stage. If you are planning to express milk into a bottle, wait until your baby is fully happy breastfeeding before you introduce the bottle otherwise he may get confused and forget how to take your nipple, or just become lazy and find sucking from the bottle easier.

Pros of Breastfeeding:

- Breast milk is tailor-made for babies
- It is free and on tap
- No bottles or other equipment needed
- Can happen any place, any time

Pros of Bottle-feeding:

- Mum is less tired
- Anyone can feed your baby

- You can measure how much your baby has taken (important for low-weight babies or those not growing well)
- Can happen any place, any time – if you plan ahead

Expressing Milk

This is a good idea for breastfeeding mums who are returning to work. It is also useful to be able to express milk so that other people can feed your baby from a bottle. You can use an electric pump or a hand pump, but whichever you choose, **wash your hands** first and follow the instructions provided with the pump. You can also use your own hand. Here is how:

- Gently massage your breast to encourage milk flow.
- Take the wider part of your nipple between thumb and other fingers to make a C-shape.
- Squeeze gently and release, building into a rhythm.
- Release the pressure and repeat, moving round the nipple if the milk is only coming in drops.
- Change breasts when the milk is dropping or ceases altogether.
- Then change breasts again before finishing each expressing session.

Expressed milk can be kept in the fridge for up to five days at 4°C or lower. It is best to keep it at the back of the fridge, not near the door. It is possible to freeze breast milk in a sterilised container. It will keep for up to two weeks in the freezer on top of the fridge, and for up to six months in a domestic freezer at −18°C or lower. Never use a microwave to defrost or warm breast milk, and once defrosted in the fridge, use it immediately.

Equipment for Bottle-feeding

If you are expressing milk or using formula, you will need some extra items of baby kit. It is best to have six baby bottles with teats and lids to get you through a 24-hour period, and sterilising equipment including a bottlebrush. Sterilising is essential to ensure you do not introduce any bacteria into your baby's tummy through his milk.

Wash your hands first then wash the bottles (teats and neck rings as well) in normal washing-up liquid. Use the bottle brush to clean meticulously into the bottom and around the neck, and ensure you rinse thoroughly under running water. Then start the sterilisation process. You can use an electric steam steriliser or similar, or a sterilising solution. Read the manufacturer's instructions and follow them precisely. Wait until the bottles have finished their cycle and cooled down before expressing breast milk into them. If you are making up a formula feed, boil the kettle with fresh clean water while the bottles are in the steriliser. You can then let it stand and cool while the bottles finish.

NANNY'S TOP TIP

Two kettles are useful while your baby is tiny. One for the household and one for him so that no one makes a cup of tea by re-boiling the water you have waited half an hour to cool.

It is best to keep a packet of sterilising tablets in the cupboard just in case you find yourself without electricity to operate your steamer. If the worst happens, however, Nanny remembers how to make sure your baby's bottles are hygienic for him to use without any gadgets.

NANNY'S DIY STERILISING METHOD

Boil a saucepan of water then plunge your washed bottles into the water, using a long-handled spoon to ensure they are totally immersed. Leave them in the boiling water for two to three minutes before taking them out and allowing them to dry on a piece of kitchen paper, necks down. Never dry a baby's bottles with a cloth. It is best to let them air dry, ensuring flies or insects cannot touch them. Then sterilise the teats and neck rings by rubbing them with salt, getting into all the corners and the tip of the teats. Rinse under cold running water and then plunge into a fresh saucepan of boiling water. Again, allow to dry on a piece of kitchen towel or muslin.

You will be sterilising bottles for at least the first year until your baby is big enough to move on to cows' or goats' milk. Sterilising for this long is based on the assumption that if your baby's stomach is not mature enough to take cows' milk until he is a year old, then his immune system is also not robust enough to withstand germs introduced by less than perfectly clean bottles. Once you are weaning, you should also sterilise your baby's cutlery and bowls for the same reasons.

Your baby will probably enjoy his breast, formula or animal milk best if slightly warm. You can warm his filled bottle by popping it into a jug of hot water for approximately two to three minutes, or use a specially designed bottle warmer. Remember, always shake the bottle once warm to disperse any hot spots. Test the temperature too by squirting a few drops on to the inside of your wrist before giving it to your baby. The perfect temperature is that closest to breast milk straight from the breast.

NANNY'S TOP TIP

Never rinse a finished bottle under the hot tap before washing and sterilising. This bakes the milk residue back on to the bottle and leaves a greasy film that sterilising may not completely remove. Rinse in cold water instead.

Formula Milk

Formula comes in powder or liquid form. Ready-made formula milk is very convenient for days out, but most families use powdered milk at home. Older mums and grandparents may suggest you make up enough feeds every morning to last you through the day, but advice changes over time. Today, Nanny has three things to say about making up formula feeds:

- Make up a fresh bottle of milk for every feed.
- If you do store milk, keep it for no longer than 24 hours and always in the fridge.
- Always follow the manufacturer's instructions.

The manufacturer's instructions will give you guidance on the ratio of milk powder to water, depending on your baby's size and age. It is just as dangerous to dilute your baby's feed too much as it is to make it too concentrated. Using too much powdered milk will not mean that he feeds less often; it will only make him ill. Too little powder will reduce his ability to put on weight properly and make him hungry.

Once you have broken the seal on the formula box, bacteria are already getting in so keep the milk powder in the manufacturer's box or an air-tight container. Using boiled and cooled tap water or bottled water for formula feeds is best. After you have boiled the kettle, leave the water to cool for no longer than 30 minutes before pouring the correct amount of water into a sterilised baby bottle. The water will have cooled to approximately 70°C, still hot enough to kill any bacteria in the milk powder. Now add a measured amount of formula powder, as instructed on the box, to the water and shake vigorously in all directions to dissolve all the powder. You should be left without any lumps in the bottle. If the bottle has cooled sufficiently, you can feed your baby immediately or run the bottle under the cold tap. Alternatively, pop it into the fridge and use within four to six hours. Always refer to your midwife for up-to-date guidelines on storing formula feeds.

NANNY FACT
Bottled water with a greater concentration of sodium than 200mg per litre is unsuitable to use for a baby.

For short trips out, carry your boiled water in a sterilised flask with the formula milk in a separate dry container, preferably pre-measured to make juggling bottle, flask and milk easier.

Once a bottle of breast or formula milk has been heated, never reheat it. This will only create germs inside the bottle. Never give a baby back a bottle he has already sucked and put aside an hour ago. It too will have started to cultivate bacteria.

Some babies are very thirsty and do not always want milk to drink. Try to encourage a little boiled and cooled water in your baby's bottle during the day. If you are breastfeeding and think your baby needs extra fluid, then give him sips of cooled boiled water on a sterilised teaspoon – he will not get confused between the teaspoon and breast the way he might if you use a bottle. Getting him used to the taste of water will be a godsend on hot days or if ever he cannot keep milk down because he is ill.

Winding

Winding your baby during his feed will help him to take more milk and keep him comfortable as he fills up. Put a muslin square or a thin towel over your clothes then place him over your shoulder close to your neck. Gently pat or rub his back until he burps. He may bring up a little milk, which is why you have the muslin in place. This is called possetting, and how much milk is regurgitated depends on the baby. If he brings up most, or all, of the milk he has taken and does this at every feed, talk to your doctor. Your baby might be suffering reflux or have an obstruction somewhere and may not be getting enough food to grow.

Effective winding takes practice by you and your baby. Apart from putting your baby to your shoulder, you could try sitting him up on your lap with one hand under the chin, supporting his head and neck, while your other hand gently rubs his back. Try a few positions until you find one that works for him.

If your baby is generally very windy, think about what might be causing it:

- Are you rushing his feed? Allow yourselves more time and try not to rush a feed simply because you have to go out.
- Is he taking in air with every suck? Teats with small holes may allow air in, so it could be time to change to 'fast flow' teats with several or larger holes.

Severe wind is also known as colic. In newborns, colic can start at three weeks and occur daily until your child is around three months old. Some families say they can set their watch by their newborn's colic – same time every evening. It is not known what causes it, or why in the first three months colic comes on in the evenings, but your job is to see your newborn through this rough patch. Above all else, stay calm. Talk to your health visitor if you are worried there may be something wrong, but if she assures you that your baby is well, then all you can do is offer comfort. Movement sometimes helps both baby and you, so pick him up, cuddle him and move around; maybe even take him for a walk. The motion of the pram may shorten an episode of colic. He might find some relief in sucking your little finger or a dummy. There are traditional and alternative remedies on the market for colic such as gripe water. On the whole, these do not work, but at least as his carer, you feel you are doing something. If you do opt for gripe water, then take medical advice first.

NANNY'S COLIC HOLD

Place your baby face down along your forearm with his tummy nestled into the heel of your hand, his bottom supported in your hand and his head resting on your arm. The slight pressure of your wrist into his tummy may give some relief.

DUMMIES AND THUMB-SUCKING

All babies love to suck. This may be comfort-sucking at your breast after feeding. If so, remember to stop it before you get sore. A baby might suck his thumb or you might decide to give him a dummy.

About Dummies

- You can take a dummy away when you want.
- It can help protect your baby against cot death (see below).
- A good dummy does not cover the entire mouth; it is designed with breathing holes in the surrounding ring.
- Only introduce a dummy to a breastfeeding baby once feeding is established at around one month old.
- Start withdrawing the dummy between six months and a year.
- Never dip it in anything sweet.
- Always sterilise it as you would all bottles.
- If it falls out while asleep, do not replace it.
- If the dummy is refused, do not force your baby to take it.
- It might cause dental problems later in life if used too long.
- It might delay speech because your baby cannot babble if always sucking.

Many parents and carers do not like to see a baby constantly sucking a dummy. However, the latest research by the Foundation for the Study of Infant Deaths (FSID) shows that a baby who is settled off to sleep with a dummy is provided with a certain level of protection against cot death than a baby who sleeps without one. Experts are still examining the reasons why this may be so.

When choosing a dummy, look for the latest designs and safety features. They now come in age stages, so ensure you choose one that is right for your baby's age. As your baby's mouth grows, so do dummies. The modern dummy comes with lots of holes and 'butterfly' mouth shapes to go over the lips, which are hollow. This is so that your baby cannot choke if by accident he does manage to get the whole dummy into his mouth. Never tie the dummy to your baby – he may strangle himself with the ribbon. A safe and well-designed dummy never has a hole to thread a ribbon through, although some are designed with a clip to attach to your baby's pram or coat.

About Thumbs

- It's harder to stop your child from constant sucking when they suck their thumb rather than a dummy.
- A thumb comes with a normal set of germs and helps to build a healthy immune system.
- No known protection offered against potential cot death.

NAPPIES

Whether you choose disposable nappies or reusable, washable ones is up to you. Only you can decide which suits your family best. Both have pros and cons, and both types of nappy are perfectly fine for your baby. If washing nappies fills you with dread, it is worth investigating a nappy laundry service in your area. A terry or fabric option could work for you if you do not fancy spending a lot of money on disposables (see page 29). There is little difference in how your baby wears his nappy or how you put it on him.

Nanny's Nappy Routine:

- Wash your hands.
- Lay out lukewarm water and cotton wool balls close to hand but outside kicking or grabbing distance.

- Have an open nappy sack or sani-bucket within arm's reach.
- Lay your baby on his back sideways on to you – this will avoid you being in the firing line of anything spontaneous.
- Remove the soiled nappy and use the front to wipe your baby's bottom, working from front to back (you might want to give a baby boy a second or two in the fresh air with his opened nappy hovering above his penis because he is likely to wee in the cooler air without his nappy).
- Roll up the soiled nappy and place in the sack or bucket (if you are using washable nappies, remove the soiled disposable liner before putting the rest of the nappy in the sani-bucket).
- Dip a cotton wool ball into the water and start to clean his bottom, always wiping in a front to back direction. Do this for boys and girls alike. Ensure you have cleaned all his creases and folds.
- When cleaning, never pull back the foreskin on a boy, and for girls, do not delve too far into the vulva. In either case you may introduce bacteria, so don't tug or pry.
- Keep wiping, each time using a clean cotton wool ball until totally clean.
- Pat his bottom dry with a clean towel.
- Allow to kick freely for a few seconds.
- Apply a nappy barrier cream if he has any redness or areas of rash (Nanny does not advise talcum powder because it cakes in his creases and remains damp).
- Lift his ankles carefully in one hand and place a clean nappy under his bottom with the other.
- Wriggle the clean nappy into place, ensuring enough is at the back and front (some babies are high riders, preferring their nappy up round their middle).

- Point a boy's penis downwards to avoid leaks above the waistband.
- Fasten the nappy with its sticky tabs or with nappy fasteners.
- Make sure your baby is safe in his cot or on the floor.
- Wash your hands.

NANNY'S TOP TIP

Remove a cardigan or other woollen top when changing your baby. Wool harbours unseen specks and germs, and can be unhygienic. Wear a plastic apron to cover you up instead.

Fabric Nappies

There are lots of modern versions of the traditional terry square. They come with Velcro fastenings rather than nappy safety fasteners. It is worth checking out these options before you settle on your choice of nappy. You might decide to alternate using disposables for days out and fabric nappies at home where it is easier to dispose of them and their contents.

No practical book of childcare would be complete without advice on how to fold a proper terry nappy – you never know when you might be caught short and need to revert to a muslin square to tide you over until you can reach a supermarket.

NANNY'S TOP TIP

Close any Velcro fastenings on baby clothes and waterproof pants before putting them in the wash. This stops them attracting fluff.

HOW TO FOLD A TERRY NAPPY

Take the square nappy and fold two corners into the middle to make a kite shape. Fold the wider point into the middle and the long point into the middle.

Place your baby's bottom in the middle and do up with nappy safety fasteners. Always place nappy fasteners horizontally, never vertically, because if for some reason they did come undone, they will not dig into your baby's tummy when he moves around.

Changing Kit

Nanny's grab and go nappy-changing kit for trips out includes:

- 6 nappies (and liners if using washable nappies)
- small pot of nappy cream
- 6 nappy sacks
- wet wipes for baby's bottom and your hands
- antiseptic hand spray

To avoid catastrophe next time you go out, get into the habit of always replenishing your nappy travelling bag when you return home, and keep it by the front door so that it truly is 'grab and go'.

BATH TIME

For tiny babies, bath time is all about cleaning and soothing before bed. In the first months, you do not have to bathe your baby daily; he probably does not need it and might not like the sensation of being naked or chilly until he can maintain his temperature better. Most babies come to enjoy bath time and by the time he is sitting up unaided, it will probably have developed into a messy and splashy end to the day.

You can use your own bath or a baby bath to bathe your infant, but ensure you are in a comfortable position and not stretching too far if using a large family bath. Your baby will resemble a slippery eel once wet and you need to keep a firm hold of him. Whatever type of bath you use, the technique is the same:

- Ensure the bathroom is warm.
- Add cold water to the bath first then top up with hot water until warm and approximately 5 cm deep.
- Test the temperature with your inner wrist.
- Place baby's towel, any creams and fresh clothes in arm's reach.
- Remove all jewellery and watches.
- Undress your baby and wrap him in his towel. Hold him firmly with his head supported in the crook of your elbow and his body tucked against your body and along your forearm (keep his nappy on while hair-washing).
- Wash his hair first. Use your other hand or a small container to pour bath water over his head, minding his eyes. He will not need baby shampoo for the first few weeks unless your health visitor has recommended you use it for cradle cap or similar.
- Dry his head with gentle pats, taking care around his fontanelle, the soft spot on top of his head.
- Once his hair is dry, unwrap him, remove his nappy and

slowly lower him into his bath, giving him time to become accustomed to the water.

- Support him with your arm behind him and let him lie back into the crook of your elbow. Your hand should be able to reach round him to keep firm hold of his arm furthest away from you.

- He does not need baby bubble bath in the early days so gradually wash him by pouring handfuls of water over him. When you are more confident, you can turn him over and let him have a moment to kick.

- **Never leave your baby or child in the bath alone for any reason, however shallow the water.**

- Never top up the bath with hot water while the baby is in it.

- Once clean, take him out and pat him dry. Do not rub his skin.

- Dress him to keep him warm once all his folds are totally dry.

NANNY'S TOP TIP

If you put your baby's babygro on the radiator to warm, remember the poppers are sometimes made of metal and can be burning hot. Check the poppers before you get him dressed.

If you are staying somewhere and the bathroom is not warm enough, it might be a good idea to bathe your baby first, then wash his hair. He loses a lot of body heat through his head and if it is still damp when he gets into the bath, he might not be able to keep warm.

Not all babies enjoy having their hair washed. Rather than spoil his bath time, you could try washing his hair only so that he does not equate bathing with hair-washing.

Advice on caring for the umbilical cord varies between health-care regions. The most important advice midwives give is to keep the cord area clean and dry, gently cleaning with fresh cooled boiled water and a non-fibrous pad. Some health experts offer new babies antibiotic powder to maintain a healthy button stump; it all depends on where you live, so it is best to take the latest advice from your midwife before you leave hospital. If you notice any discharge, bleeding or unusual or unpleasant smell, contact your healthcare specialist immediately.

As your baby grows and becomes more active, he will be grub-bier at the end of the day. You might want to introduce a mild baby bubble bath at this point, and he might like some toys to play with like pouring cups or a rubber duck. Make sure all soap products are 'tear free' to avoid sore eyes if the suds get in.

If your bathroom or his bedroom is warm enough, your baby might enjoy a massage after his bath, but remember to keep him warm because tiny babies can struggle to keep their body temperature just right. Post-bath is also a good opportunity to check your baby's skin for rashes or other irritations.

Once he is older, you can share the bath with him if you wish. It can be fun playtime together and introduces the idea that nudity is not a problem.

Nanny has one rule for older babies in the bath – leave the taps alone. Instil this rule from day one to avoid calamities – scalds or floods – later on.

Topping and Tailing

In the first days when your infant is not bathing daily, you can top and tail him on the days in between. This means washing his face, hands and bottom. Washing his neck folds and behind his ears will remove any dribbled milk before it becomes stale.

- Wash your hands.
- Use cooled boiled water in a bowl.
- Take a piece of cotton wool, dip it into the water and wash his eyes first if needed, wiping gently from the inside corner to the outside.
- Discard the cotton wool, and do the other eye with a fresh piece.
- Use a clean cotton wool ball for each cleaning motion across his face, neck, behind his ears and both hands.
- You can clean his bottom with clean cotton wool balls for each wipe, paying particular attention to his creases, and remember the 'no tugging, no prying' advice from nappy changing.

Nanny's Nursery Rules:
- Outdoor shoes off in the nursery
- Long hair tied back
- Fingernails short and clean
- No rings, watches or bangles
- Remove all dangly earrings and necklaces
- Damp dust the nursery every day (see below)
- Ventilate the nursery and air your baby's cot daily

Norland Nannies are trained to include the nursery rules in their morning routine. It may sound a lot to think about, but the rules on no jewellery are for your safety as well as the baby's because tiny babies love to grab. Short nails and hair back is for hygiene as well as to stop you accidentally scratching your baby or a stray hair getting wrapped round his fingers. To damp dust, moisten a duster instead of using polish and wipe down all nursery surfaces every day. Airing his room and cot will help to keep him healthy, so pull his cot covers back and throw his windows wide open while you are showering and he is safely in his cot or basket near you.

GROOMING

Regular grooming will keep your baby in tiptop condition. Keep a check on his finger- and toenails. In the first months, his nails may grow as quickly as the rest of him so it is worth buying a pair of round-nosed baby scissors. Cutting his nails will be easier after he has had a bath when they are softer. To cut nails safely, gently hold his finger or toe between your thumb and index finger. Very gently press down on the nail area while you are cutting with the other hand. This method will help to stop you cutting too low and hurting him. Always take it slowly and gently until your confidence builds.

There is no need to clean your baby's ears with a cotton bud on a stick. Nothing should be poked into his ears or nose. Simply use the damp corner of a muslin square if he needs a bit more attention in these areas.

Cradle Cap

This common and harmless condition may occur in the first days of life and can last for some months or even the first two years. It is nothing to worry about, but do ask advice from your baby health specialist if it does not clear up in the first months or starts to spread. Gentle daily washing in clean warm water is recommended to loosen the scales. You can also massage a small amount of unperfumed baby oil, or olive oil, into the scalp at bedtime. This will help loosen the scaly patches, which you can gently brush out with a soft baby brush. A mild baby shampoo might help, but avoid any shampoo that has a groundnut or peanut oil base. Seek medical advice if you think the cradle cap is becoming inflamed or infected.

Brushing Baby's Teeth

Brushing your baby's first tooth is a real milestone in his development. Cleaning starts from the moment the first white sliver appears above his gums. Your baby will take around two and a half years to gain a full set of twenty teeth, but the sooner you start to care for them, the better for him. Choose a soft toothbrush and baby toothpaste specifically made for his age. Both come in age ranges for first teeth, 0–6 months, toddlers' teeth and so on. Squirt a pea-sized amount of toothpaste on to his brush and gently massage his tooth, or teeth, and gums. If you sit him on your lap with his back to your chest, this will help you to hold him safely while also holding his head up from underneath his chin. Try not to let him swallow the toothpaste, and rinse with cold running water on his brush.

NANNY'S TOP TIP

If you are carrying your baby up or down stairs, never carry anything else. Keep one hand for baby and one hand, on the rail, for you.

CRYING

Crying babies are distressing for parents and carers alike. It means that something is wrong and your baby cannot solve the problem for himself. You know your own baby best, so you know if he cries because he does not like his bath, or does not like getting dressed. If, though, the reason for his crying is not immediately obvious, then run through a mental checklist before you start to think more laterally.

Nanny's Crying Checklist:
- Is he hungry?
- Is he thirsty?
- Is he overtired?
- Is he wet or dirty?
- Is he cold or too warm?
- Is he bored?
- Is his bedding twisted under him?
- Is he in pain with tummy ache or wind?
- Is he lying across a limb or stuck in any way?
- Check his temperature.

If he is still crying once you have run through your checklist and tried to solve everything, try distracting him with a toy or a song, or show him a new book, and give him a cuddle. Crying is a natural state for young babies; it is the way they communicate. However, if you think his crying stems from something serious, then seek medical advice immediately. If you find you are not coping, first take a breather with a cup of tea and try again. If you have tried everything and really do not feel you can continue, seek advice and help for both of you.

SLEEP

When there is a newborn in the house, sleep is essential for all your family. Your baby will sleep for around 18 hours a day in the first few weeks of life. However, as he will need night-time feeds, you could start to feel like you have not slept at all unless you plan and organise your new sleep patterns.

In the first weeks, he will sleep when he wants and wake for feeding. He may wake two or three times during the night for milk feeds, and it may take you an hour to change him and feed him and get yourself back off to sleep. If so, you are going to need to top up on sleep during the day to function properly and stay well. So when he next falls asleep, pop him in his carrycot or basket in the sitting room beside you and get some sleep yourself. Never fall asleep with him cuddled up to you on the sofa or in an armchair. If you are dog-tired, you run the risk of letting go and dropping him, or he may overheat. He is safer on the floor in his carrycot or basket, and you will sleep more restfully too. You may think that his sleep times are for you to dash around cooking and cleaning or washing up bottles. Some of the time this is true, but take time for yourself. You need to sleep.

Safe Sleeping

When putting your baby into his cot or basket, there are two rules: **feet to foot** and **on his back**. This means your baby sleeps with his feet at the foot of his cot, basket or carrycot. This gives him lots of air space around his head and, most importantly, he cannot wriggle under his blankets and be unable to wriggle back out. He should sleep on his back at all times. When he is older, he may roll over, but in the first months, put him down only on his back. Research has shown that babies who sleep **feet to foot** and **on their backs** have a reduced risk of sudden infant death syndrome (SIDS), or cot death. Make safe sleeping part of your daily routine.

Making up a Cot:

- Mattress protector to cover mattress
- Fitted sheet on the mattress
- Flat sheet and cotton or wool-mix cell blanket on top
- Tuck the sheet and blanket into the bottom of the mattress
- Tuck in square corners
- Fold back one corner to make it easy to pop your baby underneath

Remember, no pillow, quilt or duvet for a baby under one year. Think about adjusting your baby's covers for the season: just a sheet with his babygro for a hot summer and maybe two blankets in the winter. Always check his room thermometer and remember not to make him too warm, particularly if you keep the central heating on all night when it is cold.

A newborn will probably sleep in his babygro under his bed linen. He should never sleep with anything on his head. Some families use a sleeping bag instead of sheets and blankets. These padded sleeping bags have dungaree-style shoulder straps and poppers to fasten them. Safe-sleeping experts recommend them to stop babies from wriggling under their covers, but they may also stop an older baby who is able to move independently from getting out of his covers if he is too hot. If it is a hot night or your baby is feverish, it might be best not to use a sleeping bag until it is cooler or he is well again. Once he is at the wriggling stage, he should be able to kick his covers off to regulate his own temperature.

Sleeping bags come in different warmth ratings, known as togs, so check when you are buying that you have the correct tog rating for the season and the sleeping bag is made from a natural fabric. Your baby may wear a long-sleeved babygro inside the sleeping bag to keep his arms warm, but always check the instructions with the sleeping bag for guidance on bedtime clothes and room temperature.

The safest place for your baby to sleep for the first six months is in his own cot in your room. Take him into your bed to feed him or for a cuddle, but put him back into his cot afterwards and do not fall asleep with him snuggled up to you. You might roll over and squash your baby in your sleep, and he may also have trouble regulating his temperature close to his parents' bodies underneath their heavy duvet.

Nanny's Safe Sleeping Checklist:
- Feet to foot
- On his back
- Room temperature 18–20°C
- Ventilate the bedroom
- Appropriate night clothes for temperature and age
- Dummy to fall asleep, recommended by Foundation for the Study of Infant Deaths (FSID)

Depending on who is getting up for work in the morning, it helps to take turns at the night-time feeds so that one person does not become exhausted. This is harder to achieve if you are breastfeeding, but you might consider night-time bottles of expressed milk so that your partner can share the feeds. Remember, only introduce a bottle once your baby is an expert breastfeeder.

Prepare your bedroom for night-time feeds and nappy changes. Get into the habit of laying out your changing mat with a nappy and cotton wool balls and a flask of warm water for bottom cleaning before you get into bed. Likewise, if you are formula feeding, a bottle of water with the milk powder already measured out in a separate container can quickly be mixed together and warmed in the remaining water in the flask. Some parents say they can change a night-time nappy with their eyes closed. Nanny does not recommend this; being organised is her trick to getting herself and baby back off to sleep quickly.

Once your baby is older and more active, his daytime waking periods will be longer and full of new activities. At this point, you will find he is sleeping without so many interruptions at night and so your need for daytime naps should decrease. At around six months, it is probably time to introduce a proper bedtime routine that will become part of your day for some years to come. (See Chapter 3 for tips on a good bedtime routine.)

Nanny gives her charges as much fresh air as possible, and this includes while they are asleep during the day. Put your baby outside sleeping flat and **on his back** with his **feet to foot** in his pram. Make regular checks on him for temperature and safety, but he will sleep all the better for being outside – except when it is foggy or in extreme weather conditions. A cat net for his pram is essential to stop animals from climbing in with him; a parasol or sunshade should be used in summer if you cannot park the pram in the shade. If he wakes up, leave him to watch the sky and trees. It is all part of the learning and resting process.

In the nursery, you may be tempted to hang blackout curtains, particularly for those light early summer mornings. Nanny does not recommend this. You do not want to raise a fussy sleeper. You want a baby who can sleep anywhere, any time, in any conditions. Also, creeping around the house after he has gone to bed, not flushing the loo or turning the radio off will not help in the long run. You want a calm atmosphere for your baby to go to sleep, but life in the rest of the house goes on.

NANNY'S TOP TIP

If you want to use a menthol vapour oil to alleviate coughs and blocked noses while your baby sleeps, put a few drops on to a muslin square and place it underneath the bottom sheet. This avoids direct contact and possible irritation to your baby's skin, and still works its magic.

Sleep Problems

Once your baby is six months or so, he may be sleeping through the night, but every now and then something happens that may cause him to have a few nights' disturbed sleep. Go with this. It may be caused by a growth spurt and he is waking because he is hungry, or he may simply be 'going through a phase'. Whatever it is, remember babies *do not* manipulate their parents, so he is crying because something is wrong. Run through Nanny's Crying Checklist (see page 37) to try to solve the problem. If your baby is finding sleep tricky, speak to your health advisor before using any medication.

Whether the crying is for one night, several nights or many times over many nights, rest assured that the sooner you tackle the problem, the quicker you will resolve it. Nanny does not advocate any form of sleep discipline, so techniques such as controlled crying and gradual retreat are out. If your baby is waking and crying, something is wrong. If your pre-schooler is waking and needs you, something is wrong, even if you think he is trying it on. Offer reassurance and possibly a sip of milk or water. Sit by his cot for a few moments and then slip away back to your own room. If all else fails and only a cuddle will do, there is nothing wrong with snuggling down together until he goes off to sleep again, when you can return him to his cot; after all, parents need sleep too. Sharing with mummy or daddy need not become a habit if you can quickly solve the problem of what is waking your baby.

If your baby has been sleeping through the night and is now waking, is he getting too much daytime rest? If so, try reducing your baby's nap times during the afternoon, or getting him off an hour earlier. If your baby is waking at night and wants milk, but you are certain he is not hungry, then try reducing the amount of milk you give him. With this technique you are trying to break the link between waking and being fed back to sleep. As your baby becomes more active, he will need more exercise to burn off his newfound energy. Games he can achieve sitting up with cushions or unaided will give his brain a workout before bed. Try a longer story with actions or more complex pictures to look at to get your baby ready to sleep.

Finally, if your instincts are telling you something is wrong, then follow up Nanny's advice with a visit to the doctor.

Teething

Teething can also cause disturbed sleep. Some babies start teething within weeks of being born; others are still displaying a full set of gums on their first birthday. Whenever your baby breaks his first tooth, it has the potential to be an uncomfortable time for all of you. Because teething generally affects the older baby, you will find it discussed in greater detail in Chapter 3.

Getting Help

For some families, lack of sleep becomes a real problem. At this stage, it is best to seek help rather than struggle on. A night off can work wonders to restore your energy, so ask a parent, sister or friend if they could care for your baby for a night or two. You will be surprised how rested you will feel after a full night's sleep. Alternatively, you could investigate the services of a maternity nurse.

Maternity Nurses

Maternity nurses can be fairy godmothers for sleep-deprived families. Many Norland Nannies are trained maternity nurses as well, and this means they start working with families from the moment a baby is born. They might accompany you home from hospital; others work nights only to give parents a chance for some sleep. Whether she is with you full-time or just for a handful of nights, a maternity nurse is trained to advise, give practical assistance and help you to settle into a routine that works for all of you. If you are thinking of employing a maternity nurse, there are a few things to consider:

- Do you want her to live in or visit daily/nightly?
- How many sessions can you afford? Does she have a minimum weekly commitment?

- What extra jobs might she be happy to offer? (Some nurses will care for siblings or cook.)

If you have employed a maternity nurse to help you from day one, you have probably had time to vet her properly and discuss how you wish to work together but maternity nursing agencies can provide a nurse at short notice for exhausted parents who want to take a breather.

Maternity nurses are particularly helpful for families with twins, triplets or more. Their experience in breastfeeding, bottle-feeding and sterilising, general baby hygiene and keeping on top of your baby's laundry is invaluable to any new family, however many babies you have had.

If you do decide to have a maternity nurse, do not be shy of asking her to do the household chores while you spend fun time with your baby. That is what she expects and is employed to do. There is one legendary Norland maternity nurse who not only does all of the above, but she leaves the family's freezer stocked full of home-cooked meals, enough for an entire month!

So, confidently settled into your new family routine, it is now time to introduce your baby to some of the exciting things you and your partner did before the little one arrived on the scene.

CHAPTER 2
globetrotting nanny

Mary Poppins always flew using her umbrella with help from the east wind. These days, nannies have to travel a little more conventionally – by trains, planes, cars and the occasional super yacht. Travelling with a nanny to care for your family takes all the hassle out of globetrotting. This chapter will reveal Nanny's secrets of successful travel with children, as well as give top tips on how to entertain a young family on a long-haul flight, road trip or train journey. So, whether you want to take the children on a weekend's camping break or trekking in the Himalayas, this chapter will ensure that you have a memorable trip rather than a holiday from hell.

It's All in the Preparation

Once you have children you will soon realise that dreams you once had of an exotic Kenyan safari with your happy awe-inspired children in tow might have to be adapted – just a little. However, many people do take their children on round-the-world yacht trips, overland through Africa and skiing in Chile, but it rather depends on what sort of parents you are and what your budget is. Travelling with young children is certainly a challenge, and there's no point in denying that it will sometimes be stressful, but as long as you are prepared for the rough and the smooth, taking a newborn or toddler with you on holiday adds a new and exciting dimension to any trip. If they get used to travelling now, they will be more adaptable little travellers when they are older.

One thing is essential to ensure your holiday runs smoothly and that's preparation. Nanny does not prepare for a journey in isolation; her tried and tested method is to include the children in all the planning and turn it into an adventure for everyone. The first step with toddlers and older children is to show them in an atlas where they are going. An excellent way to wile away a few hours is to help them draw their own map with drawn or cut-out pictures of things you might see on the way. If you are travelling by car or train, plot lunch and toilet stops with them; show them where the parks are or interesting cities where they might like to stop.

For older children, always make sure they have their own little travel bag or small backpack with pocket books, toys and some notepads and crayons. Encourage them to think about the things they need – their special beaker or favourite teddy. Get them to pack their own bag.

So once the children are packed, it is time to consider what you need for the journey ahead.

NANNY'S MAGIC TRAVEL BAG

Mary Poppins always travelled with her famous carpetbag. Nanny may not be able to pull lamp stands and mirrors from hers, but she knows that a correctly packed travel bag is an essential accessory for any globetrotting parent. Nanny's travel bag is packed with everything she will need for the trip and everything the children will need to start enjoying their holiday from the moment they arrive. No nanny or well-prepared parent should leave home without these basic items.

Nanny's Travel Bag Checklist:
- Changes of clothes
- Large pack of wet wipes
- Tube of antibacterial gel handwash
- Nappies

- Nappy creams
- Small hand towel
- Favourite foods
- Dummy
- Ziploc bags
- Age-appropriate paracetamol
- Shawl or sarong
- Spare shirt for you
- Power adaptor
- Flat-pack bag or pillowcase

Changes of Clothes

These range from six for a baby per day to just a few for older children. Layers are always a good idea for toddlers as you can peel off anything too dirty; always remember to keep a clean top layer to put back over anything too grubby to be on show. Removing jumpers at meal times means you will always have something presentable for your arrival.

Wet Wipes

We all know these are essential and not just for babies' bottoms. Antibacterial wipes are a godsend on long-haul flights for hands and toilet seats.

Nappies

Only you know how many nappies your baby can get through in a day. Always overestimate, adding on a few for safety so that you will travel with sufficient nappies to cover your trip, delays and tummy upsets. If you are travelling by car or train, having a good supply is less of an issue because you can replenish your stocks. However, if you have a baby who knows when their brand of nappy has been changed, plan ahead and research if they are available at your destination.

NANNY'S TOP TIP

If your child is toilet-trained, remember that he might not remain dry at night in strange surroundings. Take night-time 'special holiday nappies' to avoid embarrassment, and a plastic mattress cover too.

Towel

A small hand towel can serve as a changing mat, a drying towel or even a privacy screen for older children who are changing into pyjamas on an aeroplane.

Favourite Foods

If you are expressing or your baby is on formula milk, remember to take enough sterilised bottles and milk powder with you. Allow for delays, spills and refused milk simply because your baby is out of routine. Airlines will supply baby food and children's meals but don't expect your child to eat them. Always make sure that you can magic a cracker, box of raisins or piece of fruit from your bag. Check with your airline what you can carry in your cabin baggage.

Ziploc Bags

You thought these small plastic bags were just for keeping foods fresh, but they are lifesavers for anyone presented with a half-chewed sandwich or a Lego set broken into small pieces. They have been used as airtight containers to ensure dry pyjamas on jungle holidays and as an emergency potty for a toddler caught short when the plane toilets were engaged. Watertight, airtight and odour-tight, they are a must for every travelling family.

Paracetamol

Ensure you have age-appropriate pain relief with you for your journey. You may not be able to find a brand you recognise and trust abroad, and airlines do not carry it on their flights.

Shawl or Sarong

This is an essential item for all journeys. It can be a sling for a baby, a blanket, a curtain over a carrycot to block out plane lights, a screen to play peekaboo, a tent for an older child, and a dress for a little girl who has wet herself.

Power Adaptor

Having one of these is particularly useful for car and train travel with babies. A travel bottle-warmer and steriliser are handy when you stop at restaurants or if your train carriage has a power socket; and a power adaptor will recharge life-supporting games devices for older children.

The first rule of travelling with children is pack as lightly as possible, stowing any non-essential items in your main luggage. The second rule is think about what is going into your Nanny travel bag and ask yourself if it is multi-purpose. For example, a handkerchief becomes a finger puppet, a teddy's parachute and a sun

NANNY'S TOP TIP

Baby and toddler mess has a horrible habit of getting everywhere, so take an old blouse or a man's shirt to wear over your clothes on an aeroplane journey. You can remove it just before you walk down the airline steps fresh and clean to begin your holiday.

hat. Be sure to have enough of everything to cope with delays, sickness and constant spills down clothes. On a long-haul flight, a bag with a square or rectangular base is best, such as a cool bag. This is much easier to place on the floor in front of your seat, and will keep bottles and beakers upright.

Your aim is to arrive at your destination as though your family had travelled with a nanny to help, and that means enjoying your holiday from the moment you arrive. It is worth carrying the first day's essentials, such as swimming costumes and sun hats, in your hand luggage. Also, if the worst happens and your luggage is delayed, you are prepared for that too.

So, whether you are travelling by car, train or aeroplane, remember Nanny's mantra: be prepared, stay calm and, whatever happens, think positive. Things won't go quite as you planned, but nothing ever does with children – or travel!

Baby on Board: Flying with Children

Flying with young children may be daunting to a new parent, but if you get it right, it can become an exciting adventure. Before you decide on an airline, it is best to check what their policy is on children – some have a better reputation than others.

Nanny's Airline Questionnaire:
- What are you allowed to carry on to the aeroplane?
- Where do they seat families?
- What baby food and milk do they provide?
- What is their policy on prams and pushchairs?
- What in-flight entertainment do they provide?

Not all airlines are child-friendly. Do not expect the information you supplied when you booked to have fed through to the check-in staff. So unless you are flying first class, always remember your magic travel bag and don't be caught out. Your first question to any airline is 'What am I allowed to carry on to the flight?' The rest of your planning is based on their answer.

Where possible, Nanny tries to fly at night so the children should sleep for most of the trip. This normally works for medium-haul flights where you are not crossing too many time zones. If you are flying long haul, then you should start adapting your child's meal and sleep routines ahead of your flight. It will help them acclimatise more quickly when you arrive.

I was nanny for a well-known Hollywood actress. I flew with her child between London and the US. Knowing the time zone changes, I started what I call a 'slipped routine' with him about a week before we were due to travel. So lunch became half an hour late, working up to two hours later by the end of the week. Likewise with supper and bedtimes, allowing for a sleep-in the following morning. By the time we boarded the plane, our routine was closer to what we would be living when we arrived. I got him adjusted the same way for coming back on those trips when we stayed overseas for long periods. **Nanny Victoria**

RESERVING SEATS

Reserving seats during online check-in is essential when travelling with children. This means you can make sure that you get the right seats before you get to the airport. If you have a child under two years old, you will usually be given a bulkhead seat with a bassinet, a type of airline carrycot. Once your children are older you will have to sit with everyone else, so ask for a block together and reconfirm this when checking in.

FEEDING YOUR BABY

If you are breastfeeding it is easy to feed your baby on an aeroplane. However, if you are expressing or using formula milk, make sure you have enough sterilised bottles for the flight. Disposable ones that can be packed flat are quite useful on long-haul trips. Travelling with liquid sterilising agent is no longer possible so you will have to rely on boiling water. In this instance, ask to supervise this activity in the aeroplane galley yourself. The stewardess may have to boil the kettle, but you should be responsible for how well the bottle is washed out with boiling water. (See Chapter 1, page 21, for specific details on how to sterilise your bottles with boiling water.) You could take a large, clean plastic container with a lid and some cold water sterilising tablets to use when you arrive at your destination.

Nanny's Holiday Medical Checklist:
- Antibiotic eardrops
- Sachets of age-appropriate liquid paracetamol
- Plasters
- Cough mixture
- Wet wipes
- Address of nearest hospital
- List of your family's blood groups
- Inoculation certificates (if going tropical)
- Sick bags or nappy sacks
- Rehydration tablets suitable for your child's age
- Medical insurance

Note: all items should be age-appropriate and familiar to your child. Check with the airline about what liquids should be stowed in your hold luggage.

PRAMS AND PUSHCHAIRS

It is often a long walk from check-in to the gate, and most airlines will allow you to check in the pram or pushchair at the very last moment. To avoid damage, pack your pushchair in its own flight bag if you have one and always ensure that it is properly labelled.

If you are travelling first or business class, you should be able to carry your pushchair on to the plane and ask the stewardess to put it in the wardrobe. This is the easiest option as they return it to you as you disembark. Some companies make fabulous travel pushchairs that fold up into a small rucksack so that you can take them on the plane with you – these are very useful if you are travelling alone with your little one as you always have your hands free and have a pram from the moment you step off the aeroplane. On arrival, pick up your pushchair first so that you can pop your child into it to keep them safe while you are pulling the rest of your luggage off the carousel.

NANNY'S TOP TIP
Remember to label your child's favourite teddy or toy with name, owner, mobile number and destination. A holiday could be unbearable without your child's special toy.

AIRLINE SAFETY

If this is your child's first experience of travelling by aeroplane, everything is going to be an adventure so be extra vigilant. At the airport lay down some ground rules about how far older children are allowed to wander, although you should always have them in your line of sight. Younger children are easily lost and should be held on reins. If they are not keen, then turn it into a fun game – pretend they are the horse and you are the carriage. This usually stops complaints.

Once on board, you should check the immediate safety of the seat you have put your child in. Nanny always checks airline seats because she knows that sometimes planes aren't cleaned thoroughly between flights. Inquisitive and excited little fingers may find Biro lids, peanuts and small coins, which could be sucked or swallowed while mum is distracted. So to avoid choking or anaphylactic shock at 30,000 feet, run your fingers deep down all sides of the seats, and check under the seat and the paper rack in front of you too.

It may seem easier to put children in the aisle seats so that they can get up whenever they choose, but it is much safer for them to sit in the window and middle seats. They cannot be knocked by passing trolleys or other passengers if they are asleep and lolling into the aisle; you are in charge of who gets up and down, and how often, because no one gets past you if you are asleep; and no one can offer the children sweets, hot drinks or anything inappropriate without leaning across you first. Stewardesses will not be aware of food allergies or personal preferences. A window seat will also amuse the children for a short while before you have to delve into your magic bag.

If anything serious happens while you are on a plane, having the children in the window seats may help you get them out safely. Asking a scared child to leave their seat and push their way into the aisle is impossible. They will constantly look round to check for your reassurance, but taking each of their hands before you leave your seat and pulling them along behind you is much easier.

TRAVEL ROUTINE

A long-haul flight can involve being on the plane overnight. The best way to deal with this and small children is to maintain their routine. Just before meal times, take them all for a walk to the toilets where they can wash their hands and come back ready to eat. After supper, as the stewardesses are asking passengers to close the window blinds, take the children to the bathroom and run them through their bedtime routine – wash, teeth clean and put on their pyjamas. Following their basic home routine will go some way to convincing them it is time to sleep. A story and warm milk should settle them even if they do not immediately nod off. Repeat your normal morning routines just before the breakfast trolley comes round. If the airline is serving meals and it is the wrong time for your child to eat, ask the cabin staff to keep it aside for you and the rest of your group so that you can eat together.

NANNY'S TOP TIP

Put the children's shoes on when they are going to the toilet. On a long-haul flight, the toilet floors can get very wet and you will regret letting them go in with just their socks.

GAMES FOR AIRPORTS AND AEROPLANES

If all your planning has worked, you will have arrived at the airport with sufficient time to check in comfortably, and just enough time for the children to enjoy the shops and watch everything going on. Although no one can fully plan for delays, you can be prepared for them.

Airport games should be contained and quiet. A balloon or two in your pocket is portable fun – play catch with a toddler or volleyball with an older child. I-spy and word games (see 'Games for the Car', below) are quieter options for pre-schoolers and upwards.

Games provided by airlines nowadays are focused on their in-flight entertainment system. You may not want your child to play computer games for 12 hours straight so check what else they provide before you start to pack your own compendium.

Aeroplane gift bags for older children generally contain a note pad and pencils or crayons and a few picture games to play but these may be based on film and television products. It can be better to pack your own.

If you plan to take games on to the aeroplane, ask each child to pack their personal selection in a rucksack small enough for them to carry in a crowded plane aisle. Small games that can be played on the pull-down tray in front of you are best, and games like Lego with lots of small pieces that will inevitably fall on the floor should be avoided. Playing 'hunt the tiny toy' under an aeroplane seat is not to be recommended. Colouring books, pencils and crayons, and a pack of cards or Top Trumps are lightweight entertainment. Keep a few surprises – a new toy, some finger puppets, a story book – in your own bag so that when they get fractious, you have something to hand that will keep them going until the next meal is served.

From pre-school age upwards, scrapbooks can keep children amused throughout the flight. Start your scrapbook at home with pictures cut from the holiday brochures and maps glued into the book. When you reach the airport, your child can begin to collect airline stickers, baggage labels, menu cards and anything that catches his eye to put in his travel journal.

I travelled alone twice with the same children to the Caribbean. We started our scrapbooks at home and they continued them throughout the holiday, collecting everything from postcards to seaweed. On the flight out and the flight back, we barely got out the other games I'd packed for the nine-hour flight. **Nanny Victoria**

Sitting still during a long flight is not good for you, so you should get some exercise together, which you can turn into a fun game too. Walking up and down the aisles is good for counting rows, or remembering where the man with the red jumper is sitting, or how many people have fallen asleep. Remember a tired child is more likely to sleep, so get walking.

LANDING AND ARRIVAL

Once you hear the landing announcement, it is time to start clearing up. If you have planned properly, you will be able to walk off the aeroplane, reach your hotel and start your holiday immediately. Norland Nannies frequently carry an additional empty flat-pack bag or pillow case in their hand luggage. This means that all the debris from the flight, such as toys, dirty clothes, bottles and beakers, can be thrown straight into this bag. When you arrive at your hotel, all your luggage including the 'debris bag' can go straight to your room, and you, your family and the swimming costumes and goggles you packed at the very bottom of your carry-on bag can head to the pool.

NANNY'S TOP TIP
Keep something to suck or chew to hand at all times. Take-off and landing can be particularly painful for babies and small children, so a bottle, beaker or slices of fruit will help them through any pressure changes. Even if you don't normally use one, a dummy for under-ones can be helpful – better than ear pain.

A note on other passengers – someone will always complain about the noise and hassle of sitting near children. It helps to introduce yourself in advance to the passengers around you and explain that there may be some disturbance from 'junior' kicking the seats or crying in the middle of the night. It won't always work but sometimes it helps to get your fellow passengers on your side.

FLY–DRIVE HOLIDAYS

If you cannot take your own car seat on a flight and you are hiring a car when you arrive at your destination, then check with the car hire company when you are booking that they supply seats of a reputable make that are age-appropriate for your child.

If you can take your own car seat, remember to cover it in durable plastic sheeting or its own cover before stowing it in the hold, and let the airline know it is part of your luggage when you book your flights.

Rules of the Road

The most common long-distance journey for families will be by car. Much of the preparation you would make for a flight can be applied here too (see above). So what does Nanny suggest when you are hitting the road?

ROUTINES

Try to keep meals (and bedtimes, if you are travelling overnight) as close to your home routine as possible. If you have chosen a particular service station for its picnic area or restaurant, then stop when you get to it, even if the children are asleep or declare they are not yet hungry.

ROUTES

By the time you set off, your child should have some idea of where he is going and what route you are taking. Fun and learning go hand in hand for Norland Nannies so even a toddler can take an interest in knowing his route. Show him the symbols for tunnel, boat, picnic area and service station so that he can spot them along the motorway, and you can encourage him to count them too.

If you had time to make a map together before you left, he can count the symbols for service stations until you get to the one you have agreed to stop at; that way you will help him to understand when it is lunchtime and he might not pester you with constant questions. If there are easily recognisable landmarks, these should be on your map for your child to spot along the way too.

> I've done some long trips by car to the South of France with small children and I know the first two hours are your grace period before boredom sets in. After that I dig out the first of some small and interesting toys to hand to the back seat. They're always things the children haven't had at home: tiny notebooks and a new pencil, a small toy such as a rubber dinosaur or doll that they can make up stories with. Audio books are my other lifesaver. Put a selection in or download a few, and everyone gets to choose one in turn, including the adults. Thomas the Tank Engine incessantly for eight hours can drive you insane. **Nanny Maria**

Where possible, travel at night for long journeys. The children will sleep and the journey can be a lot less stressful, as long as you have access to some strong coffee; but of course, don't drive if you are tired.

CAR SAFETY

Norland Nannies spend a full day learning about children's car seats. Why? Because a car seat is probably the most important item you will buy for your child. Although some car seats are fitted in the car by the manufacturer, you will need to know how to fit one safely when you use hire cars on holiday. It is safer to fit child seats in the rear of the car. NEVER fit a rear-facing baby carrier in the front passenger seat. If the car is fitted with an airbag on the passenger side and you were in a collision, the airbag would strike the seat with considerable force. Always follow the manufacturer's instructions and make sure that the seatbelt passes through the correct guides on the child seat; they can be quite complicated so make sure you give yourself time to work it out. Kneel or lean on to the child seat to tighten the belt to make sure there is no slack. Always keep the instructions for the seat safely in the car. This is useful as when you are tired you might forget exactly how it goes in, or if you are transferring to a friend's car the instructions are to hand.

NANNY'S TOP TIP

At toilet stops or service stations, designate which adult is looking after which child. Children have got lost because dad thought mum was watching them and mum thought dad was.

ARE WE THERE YET? GAMES FOR THE CAR

When the children are bored with their colouring books, finger puppets, story and picture books and looking out of the window, and the inevitable 'are we there yet?' question crops up, Norland Nannies have a range of fun family games up their sleeves to keep the children occupied until the next pit stop. As well as the obvious I-spy, here are some of their tried and tested favourites.

I'm Going on a Trip

The first person says 'I am going on a trip and I am going to take …' The second person says 'I am going on a trip and I am going to take ...' (names first person's item then adds his own). It is a memory game that you can take one step further by remembering what YOU have packed. This encourages your child to remember what he has with him so hopefully he can help in not losing anything while on holiday. You can make the game more difficult for older children by giving each round of the game a theme to stick to.

Who am I?

'I am a character in a book and film. I have an umbrella, a carpet-bag and I wear a uniform ... Who am I?' If the child doesn't guess correctly, add another clue such as 'I carry a carpetbag and slide up the banisters'. Any subject can be used such as 'I have four legs, a long tail, black and white stripes and I live in Africa'. This allows you to match the game to the interests of your children. Make it more difficult for older children by being more cryptic with your clues.

Tell a Noisy Story

This is good for all ages. You tell a story but you leave key words out and replace them with noises or sounds. Your children have to shout out the missing word. For example, a story about Percival the pig might go something like this: 'Percival was an oink oink (your child shouts out what animal), and one day he was feeling very boo hoo sniff sniff (shouts out the emotion) because the farmer had not put his favourite crunch crunch (oats) in his trough that cockadoodle doo (morning).' This can go on as long as patience and imagination permit.

Car Bingo

Before you leave home, take a piece of card and divide it into squares with a ruler. From a magazine, cut out pictures and glue them into the squares, such as a sheep, a house, a church – anything you know you will see en route. Get it laminated if you have time.

On your journey your child can look out for these objects on his board and shout bingo when he spots them all. A sweet or sticker is awarded to the first player to get a full house. You can make the pictures more obscure for older children.

Car Cricket

This is one for country lanes. You are looking out for pubs; whoever spots a pub first reads its name and scores runs for the number of legs mentioned. Here's how to score: 'The Green Man' is two legs, so two runs. 'The Green Man and his Dog' is six legs therefore six runs. 'The Spreading Oak' is all out because it has no legs. 'The Slug and Lettuce' is one to argue about.

Nanny does not recommend iPods and portable DVD players for travelling children. This is family time and they would prefer everyone to be joining in. Yes, we know that's tough but this is probably the most family time you will get together, so make the most of it. If you have a range of ages in your family, such as teens and toddlers, it can be tricky. Norland Nannies make one exception when it comes to computer games in the car: when your 14-year-old has played her fair share of toddler and pre-schooler games, she should be allowed some personal time, but restrict the use of an iPod or computer game to an hour at a time.

Keep some sweets or a surprise back for those difficult travel moments. If you are travelling in a car alone with children, you can give them a packet of sweets, a comic, a book or a small toy to buy you some quiet time when you need to concentrate. As a tricky intersection stretches your patience, they can all be preoccupied while you read road signs and negotiate the traffic.

CAR SICKNESS

Some children are prone to sickness on long car journeys. While there is not much you can do to stop it if your child is susceptible, you can be prepared for the consequences. Always have the window slightly open. It helps to look at the horizon so encourage your travellers to look out for specific objects, perhaps by playing a game of I-spy. For older children, ask the chemist for an over-the-counter medicine or herbal remedy that may help alleviate the symptoms. Put plastic on the floor and an easily washable or wipeable cover on their seat and on the seat immediately in front so you can clear up quickly and easily. Remember your travel bag – lots of wipes, tissues and sealable plastic bags will be required for soiled clothes. If you know your child gets car sick, try and travel when he will be asleep – he is less likely to vomit if he is resting.

The Runaway Train ...

There are many benefits to going on holiday by rail. The children have your undivided attention, there are toilets and you can move around, which can mean more time for games and chat and less whinging. However, if you are changing trains or have a long walk at either end, you need to make sure you have minimal baggage and a collapsible buggy for toddlers. It is often best to carry everything in a rucksack as that leaves your hands free. You can sometimes arrange for assistance or porters at stations but presume that this may not happen and travel light.

Nanny is meticulous in planning for any trip, and those top tips that she gives for travel by air and car (see above) are applicable to train travel as well. However, here are a few extra essentials that will make train travel that bit easier for families:

- Allow older children freedom to move around, but set ground rules for how far and ensure they return to their seats when the next station is announced.
- Carry your own toilet roll – trains run out very quickly. You can leave the unused roll behind when you get off.

- Do not stow your heavy luggage in the rack above your children's heads, but do ensure you use this space with your smaller items to prevent other travellers putting their heavy luggage above you.
- Brief everyone on what is going to happen if you have to change trains, particularly if you are travelling abroad. Tell everyone to stay together, keep smaller children on reins and lead the way with another adult bringing up the rear if there are two of you.
- If you have a big group, count everyone and everything off one train and count them all on to the next. Most big families have a story of when they 'forgot' one of their children so some military style organisation is required!

The usual I-spy and out-the-window spotting games may be trickier to play on trains since everything dashes past so quickly, so take some easily packable table top games and cards: snap, happy families or Top Trumps will wile away a few hours.

Arriving and Settling in

Start your holiday by having realistic expectations. After a long flight, drive or train journey, everyone is going to be tired. The children will be overexcited when you arrive and all you will want to do is collapse on a sun-lounger with a relaxing drink. So split your resources – one parent should supervise the children while the other gets some rest or unpacks, and after an hour or so swap.

Remember to help your children to adjust to their new surroundings and time zone. If you have arrived in the morning with tired younger children, let them have an afternoon nap but wake them around 4pm so that you stand a good chance of getting them to bed a few hours later. Packing a plastic under-sheet is a good idea, even for children who are dry, as the change of time zone and disrupted routine may result in a wet bed.

Tropical Nanny

If you are travelling to the tropics or anywhere where health precautions are needed, you will need to take special care to protect your family. This may mean a visit to the doctor or a travel clinic before you go. You need to check if your child's immunisations are up to date; he might need extra jabs depending on what country you are visiting. Generally, you will need to start planning immunisations about four to six weeks before you leave on holiday. This is because many vaccines require a primary and then a secondary dose a few weeks later. There can be a minor reaction to some vaccines so, if you work or your children are at nursery or school, plan to have the jabs done on a Friday after school. This means that if your child feels unwell afterwards he can be at home. Most reactions to vaccines tend to happen within 48 hours so it's much better if this happens over a weekend when you are most likely to be together. If you are travelling to Africa you will need a Yellow Fever certificate for your child. Keep this safe as it is proof that they have had the vaccination. Without it you will not be allowed into some countries or, worse, have to have the vaccine at the airport.

Many parents worry about travelling to exotic locations if it means that their children require malarial prophylactics, so always check with your doctor what is required for the country you intend to visit. Your doctor will have the best advice for taking young children to malarial areas.

Always research the health advice for your holiday destination. One of the most important questions to ask is: can you swim, paddle in or drink the water? In Africa, for example, water can contain parasites that can infect people. Just because local people swim or paddle in it doesn't mean that it is safe. Always check before you go and if you don't know, don't risk it.

Even the less-adventurous traveller still needs to be aware of a few hazards. Remember that babies are particularly susceptible to changes in food and water.

DRINKING WATER

This rather depends on where you are holidaying but don't depend on a clean drinking-water supply from every tap. If you are in a country where clean drinking water may be an issue, use only bottled water for drinking, diluting fruit juices and boiling for babies' formula feeds. It is also advisable to clean your children's teeth in bottled water. If your child likes ice in his drinks, this should be made from bottled water too – do not allow the waiter to throw in some ice cubes from the bar unless you absolutely know they are made from clean or purified water.

FRUIT AND VEGETABLES

If you buy fresh produce from markets, you should wash it thoroughly in bottled water prior to eating. You may wish to steer clear of prepared salads and fruit in some hotels. Unless you know otherwise, it is advisable to err on the side of caution and take control by washing everything yourself or peeling it.

HEATSTROKE AND SUNSTROKE

These conditions can take a small child or baby unawares. Keep them covered up with long-sleeved cotton tops and trousers, as well as using a high-factor sunscreen. Remember to give your child some respite from the sun throughout the day, and lots to drink. Some buggies come with sunshades, and in some countries you can get UV nets that double as fly screens. (For more on identifying the signs of heatstroke or sunstroke and how to deal with it, see Chapter 5.) Also carry a mister spray with bottled water so you can keep everyone cool.

DUST

Small people experience a lot more dust than the average adult. Their faces are at wheel and tyre height; so if you are in a particularly dusty environment, give your child some protection. A small baby is probably best carried close to your chest in a sling rather than in his pram, and a toddler might appreciate the better view from a backpack – it will also serve to keep inquisitive fingers from scratching in the dust and picking up absolutely anything that interests them.

NANNY'S TOP TIP

Trim fingernails as short as you dare for toddlers upwards on holiday – it reduces the likelihood of germs getting under the nails and being transferred to the mouth.

There's no stopping you now ... So those are the basics for travelling with children. Armed with your *Nanny in a Book* there is now nothing to stop you from skiing, sailing or camping with your young children. Here are some of Nanny's tips on 'specialist' holidays.

Skiing with Nanny

Most ski instructors recommend that skiing is best started when children are three to four years old, but this rather depends on the child's strength, coordination and character. Many Europeans start their children skiing as soon as they can walk – that's why they tend to win at the Winter Olympics! But skiing is much easier when your children are out of nappies and have the stamina to ski for more than an hour.

If you are planning to holiday in a ski resort with your baby, be aware that many package ski companies will only take children from six months old. Make sure you pick a company that is 'baby friendly' – some aren't. Your childcare options for youngsters who will not be skiing are: a nanny who comes to your chalet or apartment, a crèche run by the resort or holiday company or a local nursery. Check what facilities there are when you book your holiday.

> I once travelled by coach to a ski resort with several young children. I packed all their toys and essentials into pillowcases, one for each child. They could put toys away and fish out their toothbrushes and pyjamas when it was time for bed, and the pillowcase turned into a comfortable cushion for stiff coach seats. When we arrived, they were already dressed in their skiwear and sped off to the slopes with their parents. I took all the luggage straight to our apartment. **Nanny Sarah**

Getting your children out on the slopes can be a complicated affair when they are under four, but if you go expecting it to be different to those 'before children' days, you will find it all much easier. Everything takes longer with children, especially on a skiing trip. Just as you get the three layers of ski gear on your wriggling, excited downhill champion, he will want to go to the toilet and you will have to take it off again. So make sure ski gear is easy to put on and take off with Velcro and zips rather than buttons or poppers. Children lose heat faster than adults so they need good thermal clothes. They will also need helmets and goggles, which can be hired or bought.

Skiing involves a great deal of organisation – trying on and hiring ski gear, queuing for ski-lift passes, walking your toddler to the crèche, all in the snow in a crowded resort, can try the patience of a saint. The key is to give yourself plenty of time: time to get dressed, time to get to the lifts, time to stop and have hot drinks to warm chilly fingers and noses. The downside of this is that you can expect the number of hours you can spend on the slopes to be reduced. If you go with this expectation you are less likely to get frustrated. Whether you have a good holiday or not rather depends on the personality of you and your children and whether as a family you can put up with the conditions. Your little ones will get cold hands and feet, ski boots can be uncomfortable, travelling to and from the ski resorts can often be long and laborious, so your child's ability to cope with long car or coach journeys and the winter conditions must be taken into account. As long as *you* remain calm and relaxed, you should be able to minimise the problems.

NANNY'S TOP SKIING TIPS:
- Make sure all clothes are easy to get on and off.
- Leave bulky pushchairs at home.
- Always choose a resort with lots of other activities – an indoor pool, a sledge park, a snow park. The older children will not want to ski all day and the younger children will want some time with mum and dad.
- Be prepared for your skiing time to be reduced – if this is a problem, one parent can ski while the other amuses the children.
- Not all children take to ski school – be prepared that one of you might have to stay with your child on the first day.
- Take a high-factor sunscreen for the children.

Ski schools, where the children have fun play sessions or ski lessons depending on their age and ability, are usually available for three-year-olds and upwards. Always check websites or with your travel company to see what facilities are available. If you choose to put your little one into ski school, check before you book that there will be an English-speaking instructor and, where possible, other children of the same nationality. Ski school is usually crowded and chaotic, so buy your children something distinctive to wear, which will make them easily recognisable when you go to pick them up. In their pocket, they should have the contact details of your hotel and mobile numbers – laminated or in a plastic sealable container. You could also avoid all the crowds and hire a private instructor for your children – they are not as expensive as you might think.

Messing about on Boats

Many sailing enthusiasts take their babies and young children sailing. You might also hire a rowing boat or go on a barge holiday, so it's always worth knowing how to ensure the safety and enjoyment of everyone on board a boat. As with all travel, making it fun or not rather depends on the attitude and experience of the parents, but there's no denying that children love messing about on boats.

The first safety rule is to make sure that all the children wear life jackets on deck, or near the harbour or marina. It helps if mum and dad set a good example by doing the same. Of course teaching them to swim, or at least be confident in the water in a life jacket, is vital, so practise at the seaside or in a pool before you go. When you are on the boat, practise jumping off and getting back in the boat in your life jackets, if it is warm enough. This is a great way to spend a hot afternoon and it increases the children's confidence if they do fall in. Children need to be told not to run on deck and to hold the guard rail at all times. Even young children can be encouraged to do this by making it a game or having a reward system where every time they use the guard rail they get a sticker, which goes towards an ice cream when you get to your destination.

Remember to pack the right clothes for the conditions in a waterproof soft bag, (no suitcases as storage on most boats is limited). Whatever the weather, warm and waterproof clothing and non-slip shoes (without black soles that mark the boat) should be the first things you pack. Don't forget essentials such as suntan lotion, sunglasses and sun hats.

With small children on board it is sensible practice that there is always one adult in charge of them while the crewing of the boat is left to others. This is especially important when carrying out careful manoeuvres such as mooring or sailing in and out of harbours. You will therefore need enough people on board to crew the boat and to watch the children.

> A travel cot wedged or lashed in a cabin can be a safe zone for babies when mooring and berthing, but always ensure someone stays with the baby throughout. **Nanny Claire**

For older children you can make the whole voyage an adventure by adding pirate hats and flags, eye patches and telescopes to your packing list. However, depending on the age and experience of your little pirates, remember that the initial excitement and novelty of being on board a boat at sea can wear off very quickly. Being on a boat can be quite static so encourage the children to get involved; under adult supervision, they can steer the boat, chart a course, row the dinghy or even scrub the deck. If they are running a pirate ship, all the better because telling them what to do is part of the game. If the boat has a cabin or saloon, it's also worth having a store of lightweight games, books and toys to keep your junior crew members entertained.

Nothing is impossible with children if you are prepared and confident. Nanny knows many parents who have taken newborns on long sailing trips and these children have grown up to be confident, independent, self-assured and often brilliant sailors. There are always risks to any adventurous activity, but you can minimise these and make sure you and your children are safe.

Camping with Nanny

Camping can be a fun holiday for the family. It's not for everyone, but if you do like the great outdoors, it can be an inexpensive adventure with children. Here are some ideas on how to make a camping trip run smoothly.

Get the children involved in the planning: the location, the food, the packing. Pick a campsite based on your family's interests: swimming and surfing, wildlife, canoeing. If it is your first time camping with children, choose a campsite with good facilities – toilets, café or games room.

If you have bought a new tent always practise putting it up in the garden or another open space before you go. There is nothing worse than trying to work out how a tent goes together when you have just arrived tired at a campsite after a long journey. Putting the tent up in the garden is a good opportunity to have a trial run with the children by camping out one night. The children will love it and you have access to everything in the house if there is a problem in the middle of the night. That said, it's a good idea to limit your first camping trip to about two to four days.

WHAT YOU WILL NEED

There are a few essentials for a comfortable camping trip: good sleeping bags or duvets, a comfortable inflatable mattress or camp beds, a travel cot for any child under two and a stove, cooking utensils and a washing-up bowl. As Nanny knows only too well, often the problem with camping, especially in the UK, is bad weather so make sure you have wellies, waterproofs and umbrellas, and whether it's summer or winter always take gloves, hats and fleeces. A range of spare clothes for the children will be useful as they will get muddy and dirty very quickly. With toddlers, make sure you take a flannel, as bathing facilities will often be limited and at least you will be able to wash your little camper down using the washing-up bowl. However, it is best to keep your expectations low when it comes to cleanliness – the week will be spent a little grubbier than normal.

Another essential is to make sure everyone over four has their own hand or head torch. Make sure they are clearly labelled or different colours so there are no rows when they get lost. Also, ensure you have a good supply of batteries as well as separate battery-operated lanterns for each tent.

Once you have been camping a few times – and presuming that going once doesn't put you off – draw up a revised list of what you need to take next time. Nanny's top camping tip is always to keep this list with your camping equipment as it makes it easier to pack next time, and you will arrive at the campsite knowing that you haven't forgotten your child's favourite beaker or the bottle opener.

For adventurous types, camping may mean no more than a tent, sleeping bags, sleeping mats and some cooking utensils, but with younger children you have to be a little more prepared. Below is a list of what Nanny believes are essentials for a proper camping trip where you and the family are travelling by car to a campsite and staying for two days or more.

Nanny's Camping Checklist:
- Tent – big is best! (but make sure it is easy to put up)
- Picnic table and folding chairs
- Beds – either inflatable mattress (and pump) or camp beds
- Pillows and bedding/sleeping bags for older children
- Stove/pans/kettle

- Washing-up bowl
- First aid kit (see Chapter 5, page 169 for list of contents)
- Clothes line and pegs
- Plastic bags – useful for rubbish, wet swim things and nappies
- Potty
- Torches and lanterns
- Warm pyjamas and plastic shoes
- Cool bags
- Can opener/corkscrew

> The family I worked for loved camping and we always took a small additional tent as a 'playroom'. They could put it up quickly, bung some cushions in with the toys and with a fanfare announce that this was the holiday den or the play tent. It also kept all those bits of Lego and cars from being underfoot in the main living tent. **Nanny Emily**

CAMP COOKING

Many campsites have kitchen blocks, but if not, you will probably do your cooking on a small stove outside. Unless you are 'camp cook extraordinaire', accept that your meals are going to be simple. For babies, bring your own home-made food in portion-sized jars – or there's always the pre-prepared food in the local shop. Make sure you bring plenty of snacks as little campers get very hungry with all that fresh air.

Nanny's philosophy on camping is that it's up to the adults to make it fun. You can help this by making the cooking into a game as well as an adventure – pretend you are explorers or have contests for who can find the most kindling, cook the best meal, or be the fastest to wash up.

CAMPING GAMES AND PASTIMES

Get the children to make nature scrapbooks or a treasure box. This is a great pastime for children of most ages so before you leave find a little box – a shoe box or toy box – for each child. They can collect things to put in it – seashells, leaves, pine cones, fossils, anything that takes their fancy. It's a great way to get them looking at their environment, but is also a wonderful memento of their trip.

Another good game is to give them an empty matchbox at the start of the trip and get them to collect as many things as possible to fit inside it – the child with the most objects in the matchbox at the end of the trip gets a prize.

Let the children stay up a bit later – it's an adventure after all – and have midnight feasts (doesn't have to be midnight!), sing camp-fire songs and take a children's astronomy book to look for stars. These may sound like old-fashioned ideas but if you leave the iPods and the games consoles behind, simple games that encourage your children to take notice of their environment are good for them, good for you and help to make a different family holiday.

There is no doubt that travelling with a new family will require considerable effort from you. It's not easy and sometimes – most times when the children are young – it will be a real challenge. In fact, a holiday may not seem like a holiday at all for parents when the children are really young. Getting holidays to work for the whole family takes time and practice but being prepared for the rough and the smooth will pay dividends.

CHAPTER 3
growing up with nanny

As your baby becomes a toddler, his individuality will grow too. He is still totally reliant on his parents and carers for survival, but he is beginning to think he is capable on his own. This is when you will need eyes in the back of your head, a sixth sense for your child's whereabouts and plenty of stamina to indulge your mobile baby and sprightly toddler in all the new adventures ahead of him. Previously, you observed him and reacted when he needed you. Now the tables have turned and he is observing you, learning from you and mimicking your every move.

So what can you expect your baby to achieve now that he is growing into a toddler? The simple answer is everything, but all at a pace unique to him. His developmental milestones – crawling, talking, eating solids – will all come when he is good and ready. As he develops into an eager little learner, parents now become teachers and safety advisors as well. So, here is what to expect, how to cope and, most importantly, how to help him get the most from this latest stage of his journey.

One Step at a Time

Parents love to compare their babies' developmental milestones and often it gets very competitive. Save the competition until your child's first sports day, and in the meantime resist becoming a pushy parent. Here are the developmental milestones – the significant new skills your baby will acquire in the next few years – and beside them are broad ranges of age when you might expect them to occur. You know your child best, so if any milestones are significantly delayed or you suspect something is wrong, seek expert advice. If your child was born prematurely, you will know from the advice you received in hospital that you should adjust your expectations according to how early your baby was born.

Nanny's Developmental Milestones:
- Supporting his head and neck alone: four months onwards
- Sitting up supported with cushions: from six months
- Hand to eye coordination – clapping, gesturing, rolling a ball: all start at around six months
- Hand grip – the pincer grip where your baby will grasp toys and smaller items with his index finger and thumb: around nine months, sometimes earlier
- First tooth: generally around six months, but can be three weeks after birth or not until nine months
- Speaking – this means anything from babbling to a full sentence requesting another drink. Listen out for 'mummy' or 'daddy' or the name of your dog: from nine months onwards
- Stopping afternoon nap: depends on how well he is sleeping at night and how active he is during the day, so go with the flow, but generally around two years
- Weaning: try this from six months after consulting your health advisor
- Feeding himself – this will happen as soon as you put a spoon within reach, but proper self-feeding takes time: at around one year your child will make a real messy go of it
- Walking: this starts out as crawling or bottom shuffling at around eight months. Some babies skip this phase

and move straight to cruising – holding on to furniture or the dog to get from one side of the room to the other. Either of these will develop into walking: usually around a year to 15 months

- Potty training: varies widely from around 18 months to 3 years, but this is definitely one milestone not to push at all

As trained childcare professionals, Norland Nannies look for a much more detailed range of abilities in any child they work with, but the above list will give parents and carers a good working guide to gauge whether their child is heading in the right direction. Take on board that if your child has an older sibling or an older friend, he may reach certain milestones early simply because he is competing in their world. On the flipside, an older child may fill in the gaps for a younger sibling, which could delay speech or other skills.

If you are the parent of twins, you will probably have noticed they are developing at different rates. This is normal; after all, they are both individuals and it is particularly important not to introduce any element of competition between them. Unless one twin begins to lapse significantly behind the other in any area of development, you should have nothing to worry about. Sit back and enjoy watching them both grow as individuals with a unique bond.

There are things you can do to encourage some of your child's new skills. Placing a toy or ball slightly out of reach will prompt your child to shuffle or roll towards it. Equally, playing games with stacking beakers will develop his hand to eye coordination; using picture books and asking questions will help him communicate by pointing. The more time you spend encouraging your child to learn through play, the more able your newly mobile explorer will become.

Table Matters and Manners

One of the great milestones for all the family to enjoy is the day your baby takes his first mouthful of real food. His expressions of surprise and hopefully glee at this new sensation will be something to cherish. Nanny has lots to say on weaning in Chapter 4, and to complement that advice, here is Nanny's guide to helping your child learn table manners fit for a prince.

Your baby's new cutlery and crockery should be plastic at first. Plastic utensils can be easily placed in your steriliser and there is no risk of smashing china. Long-handled baby spoons with very soft bowls on the end will not hurt your baby's tender mouth and you can reach him to feed him in his highchair.

Highchairs are now a necessary part of your baby's equipment. There are two main types – with and without an integral tray. Nanny prefers highchairs that pull up to the dining table and do not have their own tray. This style of highchair includes your child at the family dinner table where he will learn table manners, how to handle his cutlery and plate, and how to join in by observing you.

Remember that as he gets bolder, he will try to climb in and out of his highchair by himself. You can ensure he is safe in his highchair by using reins that anchor to the chair's fixing points. It is best to stop him from clambering into his highchair alone from the first time you witness it. You do not want him to learn the hard way by pulling it over on top of himself.

NANNY'S TOP TIP

Avoid tablecloths with small children – a toddler can be too helpful and clear an entire table with one deft swipe.

If the thought of your baby damaging an expensive dining table fills you with horror, protect it rather than excluding your child from sitting at it. A colourful rubber place mat rather than an adult table mat will prevent him from digging his cutlery handles into the wood and will stop his bowl from slipping about as he chases peas with his spoon.

From his first birthday or even earlier, he will be very interested in feeding himself and may make a grab for his spoon. If you think he is ready for this next challenge, let him have a go. Most likely he will tip his spoon upside down as it reaches his mouth. This will confirm that his hand to eye coordination really is working perfectly, and you can contain the mess with a scoop bib and a mat or newspaper placed on the floor to protect your carpet.

Nanny never lets the dinner table become a battlefield. Your baby will not respond well to being forced to eat and he may develop an aversion to meal times, associating them with difficult moods. Instead, when the signals that he is full are obvious, ask him if he is finished and encourage him to sit still until everyone else has finished too. This may sound impossible, but if you start with just a minute of his extra time now, once he is older you should have a child who will sit politely until everyone is ready to leave the table together.

Good table manners begin with consideration for everyone eating a meal together. Go through the list of people having dinner tonight with your child – mummy, daddy, older sibling. He will be learning to count as well as learning to think about others. Count with him at first, and when he is a little older ask him to count out the correct number of knives and forks from the cutlery drawer (you might wish to supervise this until you are happy he knows the rules on knives). If you show him how to lay one place setting, let him attempt the rest. You may have to adjust the odd spoon, but this is the first step to a polite child at your table.

You might set him the task of asking everyone what he or she would like to drink. If an older sibling is still using plastic beakers at the table, then your toddler might pour that drink for him and carry it to the table with your assistance. If he starts with his brothers and sisters, then remembering to offer guests a drink will be even easier.

At the table, your child will learn through observation so if he hears you asking 'please pass the vegetables' or 'may I have more meat', eventually he will do so too. If you need to correct his handling of cutlery, do this gently by asking him if you can help then turning the spoon round in his hand and adjusting his grip. If you snatch it from him, he is likely to do the same to someone else one day.

Nanny's one firm rule is: no playing with food. You can serve his meal with his sausages poking out of the mashed potato to create a hedgehog to entice him to eat, but once it is at the table, the game gets eaten.

NANNY'S TOP TIP
To get your baby to accept the spoon, open your mouth with every spoonful you feed him. He will copy you and open his mouth too.

With your child's table manners perfected at home, you can now introduce him to the world of public dining. Taking a toddler out for a meal is particularly rewarding if the waiting staff do not shy away from serving your table, and other guests in the restaurant congratulate your child on his behaviour. Who could fail to accept some of the glory for themselves? Remember, not all restaurants will accept children, so check before you book.

It is pointless expecting a toddler to sit still during a long dinner, so take along pencils and a notebook in your bag to keep him occupied once the novelty of the restaurant wears off. You can inspire his work by asking him to draw a picture of his food or daddy eating his dinner, and playing battleships is a winner with older children. If the experience of dining out suddenly overwhelms your child, it is good manners to go outside before a public meltdown ensues – you want to make sure the restaurant will have you back. Also, do clean up a little after your meal. It is not fair to expect the poor waitress working long hours to clear up additional mess. It proves you are a well-behaved family with five-star manners.

Respecting Your Toddler

Respect is Nanny's watchword when it comes to negotiating with a toddler. Your baby has always been an individual with rights and that is truly emphasised now he is more physically and mentally able. Your toddler is exploring the boundaries of what is allowed and what is not by observing you. If you show him respect, he will show you some back. It is that simple. For Nanny, body language is everything, so get down on his level by crouching or kneeling. If you are looming over him he will feel small and insignificant, and he will receive the conversation at a more serious level than you may have intended. So respect your toddler, get down at his height and make eye contact. Uncross your arms to show that you are welcoming and open.

If your toddler's behaviour has made you cross, it is better to deal with it at his height. Looking him directly in the eye will calm any feelings of anger you had because it is harder to launch into a terrible telling-off when you can see his lip trembling and his eyes welling up. You will feel more able to talk to him to figure out what is making him behave this way. If you let him, he will tell you how *he* sees the situation. Help him to calm his tears by letting him know that he is not in trouble. Give him time to get his side of the story out and then tell him how you feel. If he understands how he has made you feel, or if he has hurt another child and needs to know how that feels, you are halfway there in being able to negotiate with your toddler. Negotiation is a valuable tool to have as his opinions become more strident and self-centred. (See Chapter 8 for more advice on how to deal with your challenging toddler.)

NANNY'S TOP TIP

Do not lift a child away from something you do not want him to do. Imagine how infuriating it is to have a giant adult pick you up and deposit you somewhere else. Keep calm, get on his level and negotiate with him, persuading him to move away. Only use total removal if he is in danger.

Respecting your child is not all about tricky times. If you are going out for the day, you will sell him the idea of shopping or visiting a relative much more successfully if you are at his height. Showing him a carrot in one hand and a cucumber in the other at his level will include him in the decision of what he will be eating at lunchtime. He will understand that his opinion is respected. If you are doing something new or momentous in your family, explain to him what is happening. Moving house is a big deal for any family, but if your toddler does not understand why his toys are disappearing into boxes, how can you expect him to work with you in such a time of upheaval? So to show respect, breathe deeply and take up this mantra:

Nanny's Family Code of Respect:
- Get down at his height
- Include him in decisions that involve him
- Explain to him what is happening
- Ask him for his opinions
- Give him space and time to explain himself

If you make respect part of your family's ethos, then managing each milestone your baby encounters will be much easier.

Feet First

Because you took Nanny's advice and put your tiny baby to sleep flat on his back in his cot, basket and pram, not only did you help to protect him from SIDS but you have also given him a strong straight spine. Most probably you will now have an early walker in the family.

The first steps to walking start on a baby's bottom and knees. From about eight months, he may begin to 'bottom shuffle' or he may decide to crawl as his first mode of transport. Whichever it is, you will need eyes in the back of your head to keep up with him. Crawlers can be particularly fast on their knees so a coffee cup left on the floor may have been acceptable only a week ago, but now anything left on the floor is fair game. For families with babies who go straight to furniture cruising, vigilance is paramount. To cruise, a baby will pull himself up using whatever is to hand. Sofas and armchairs are the normal favourites, but a wobbly coffee table or fireplace are equally as attractive to the uninitiated and determined sitting room traveller. You do not have to turn your home into a padded cell, but do take a look at 'Risky Business' later in this chapter (see page 98) to help you avoid a trip to the local A&E.

Once your child is walking, life speeds up for him but will slow down for you as he tries to keep up. Do not rush out to buy shoes the minute your baby takes his first step. The soft bones in his feet

must have time to become accustomed to this new position; wait
six to eight weeks before you have his first shoes professionally
fitted. Walking with bare feet on well-vacuumed carpets is perfect
for learner walkers, and if you have cold stone floors, then socks
with rubber suckers on the bottom will prevent him slipping.

NANNY'S TOP TIP

For early morning padding about the nursery, cut the feet out
of his babygros or pop his legs out and tie the leggings loosely
round his waist to give him good contact with the floor.

Once your toddler has found his balance, there will be no stopping
him. A staggering run with wide-splayed feet will normally end in
your baby dropping to his knees or thudding to the floor on his
nappy until he can learn to stop and alter direction. Steps will be
an issue for him so show him how to negotiate them on his
bottom – it's much easier and safer. With walking comes climbing.
Your sofa might look as high as Mount Everest to him but he will
not be put off because, at this stage, everything is worth a try.
Nanny assures you, he *will* have a go. Last week you could leave
him in his carrycot or sitting safely propped up with cushions while
you nipped to the kitchen for a few seconds; those days are gone.
Now wherever you go, he must go too.

NANNY'S TOP TIP

Super-clean glass doors appear totally transparent to a
toddler. Put colourful stickers across them at his eye level to
avoid painful bumps.

You can help your toddler become a more confident walker by buying him a push-along trolley. These often come with bricks in them, which double up as stacking and early alphabet toys too. If you are nervous about him crashing the trolley into your skirting boards, then an alternative might be a stuffed toy dog on a trolley. These are softer on your furnishings, and they are still educational because you can introduce the stuffed dog to your toddler as 'his pet' and teach him to offer it a bowl of water and some food.

Sitting on the floor and getting your baby to walk between you and your partner will also aid his walking. A steadying hand is always close by, and as his abilities improve you can move further apart or introduce obstacles, like a book, for him to see and walk around. Soon, your toddler will be attempting to jump and hop, and running circles round you.

The Potty

He is up, he is off and that nappy will no doubt be slowing him down. Around this time, most toddlers are beginning to get some bladder and bowel control too. This is your chance to introduce a potty. Your life will be so much easier if this coincides with summer when your toddler can go without a nappy and do the potty dash unhindered outside. Norland Nannies are not taught strict 'toilet training' because starting too soon without the cooperation of the child results in 'toilet trouble'; instead they are taught how to encourage correct use of the potty at a time that appears right for the child. You may have heard that boys and girls learn to be clean and dry at different rates. More importantly, every child learns these hygiene skills at his own pace.

From the first day you bring the potty into the room, Nanny has four potty rules to avoid calamity:

- A potty is never a toy
- A potty has only one use – toddler toilet
- A potty is only emptied by an adult
- A potty is always emptied immediately after use

These four rules mean a toy can never be dipped into a full potty and the potty's contents can never end up being tipped into the toy basket.

NANNY FACT

You cannot force a toddler to empty his bowels to order. Push him and he will use it as his ultimate control – revenge will be his.

As with all nursery equipment, potties come in all shapes and sizes. Take your child to the shop with you and ask him to choose which colour potty he would like. If he is involved, he is more likely to want to use his new potty. A well-designed potty has:

- A wide sturdy base
- A 'tongue' at the front to help little boys not to spray
- A simple and easy-to-clean design with no hinges or lips to harbour germs

Once you have chosen your toddler's potty together, you need to find a suitable place to keep it so it is easily reached. If you have a garden and potty practice coincides with summer, then a discreet patch in the garden to site your potty might work best. Otherwise, a downstairs toilet is advisable. The upstairs bathroom can be tricky for a toddler to reach in time. If you do not have a downstairs loo, it might be best to compromise between hygiene and accessibility, and put your toddler's potty in a corner of a utility room or even the kitchen where you are least likely to have carpets. A rubber mat underneath helps to maintain hygiene if you cannot avoid carpeted floors. Wherever you and your toddler decide is best – remember to put it in the same place every day for obvious reasons!

Before children, you may have enjoyed privacy in the toilet, but it will help your toddler to understand what goes on if you allow him to observe you in the bathroom. Nanny is not advocating giving him the details, just the gist so that he can copy you on his potty.

INTRODUCING THE POTTY

Being ready to use the potty is as individual as any other developmental milestone. Your toddler may have developed regular bowel movements so you may be able to predict when to offer him the potty for the first few attempts. He may start to tell you he has wet or soiled his nappy, or point to his nappy to let you know. He may even be upset if he has soiled his nappy. All of these are good signs that the time is ripe to introduce the potty.

Your toddler will find it easier to control the muscles that operate his bowels than those connected to his bladder. For this reason, he will probably be clean before he is dry. If your toddler is generally getting used to the potty and you have found that he is waking from his afternoon nap with a dry nappy, then he is showing signs of some bladder control. Ask if he would like a wee before his nap and if he would like to sleep without a nappy. If he is keen, sit him on the potty and remember to tuck a boy's penis downwards to avoid splashes. If he urinates, then you are on the road to success, but if he is reticent, then pop a nappy on him; and if it proves to be dry when he wakes, ask if he would like to use the potty and then sit him on it. His bladder will almost certainly be full and a successful wee now with little cajoling and a reasonable level of praise could mean that tomorrow he asks for the potty himself.

It is important not to show disgust or hold your nose when you pick up his full potty. This might put him off using it and make him feel dirty. After all, what is in it is his. Some children can become very upset if they see you flushing their potty contents down the loo; they may feel you are getting rid of a part of them. So until he understands better, let him observe the clearing-up process and explain what is happening. Also, take pride in your little one that he is a big boy now and can use a potty successfully, but do not overdo the praise. Going to the toilet is a natural part of life so give reasonable encouragement and small rewards – a star chart is a great way to promote use of the potty.

As for bottom wiping, this is your responsibility until your toddler is totally in command of his bowels and the potty. Remember to wipe front to back for boys and girls, and it will help if your child leans forward and touches his toes while you do the necessary.

Nanny's Potty Emptying Routine:
- Ensure your child is safe or beside you before you take the potty to the bathroom.
- Cover the potty with a sheet of kitchen towel or similar to avoid spills on the journey.
- Tip the contents into the loo and wipe round with toilet paper.
- Wash out the potty thoroughly using disinfectant and hot water.
- Leave the potty to dry.
- Clear up any spills around the potty's floor space with disinfectant.
- **Wash your hands and your toddler's thoroughly.**

Instilling hand hygiene after every potty or toilet trip now will result in you having a clean child for the future when your pre-schooler is doing it for himself.

There are helpful products on the market to make the dash to the potty more successful, but Nanny recommends opting for the straight-to-pants approach; it is cheaper but expect a lot of wash-ing. Buy cotton pants and try to include your child in the purchase. Many have characters on them, which might encourage him to wear them if you let him choose. Remember, you are going to need a lot of them, so stock up.

Regular reminders to use the potty are going to become common parlance until your toddler is potty-confident. Encourage him to use the potty every time you go to the loo and remember to leave enough time for a potty session if you are heading out shop-ping. Everything takes just that little bit longer now you have a toddler in the family.

OUT AND ABOUT

Public toilets are not great for little ones, although increasingly the bigger department stores and children's shops offer toddler-sized toilets. Check for cleanliness before you use them and always super-vise your toilet novice. For long journeys, a port-a-potty is great. This is a plastic potty seat with little collapsible legs and plastic bags to act as the potty bowl. They are easily erected on roadsides and lay-bys, and the contents of the plastic bag are readily disposed of. You could just go 'al fresco' but discuss as a family whether you feel a wee in a wood or field is appropriate. You might find it easier to relax your rules about outdoor weeing until your toddler gains more bladder control.

I helped a mum who had a little boy of two and a half who was already potty trained. Everything was great until suddenly he stopped going in the potty and consequently there were many pairs of pants in the bin. I asked his mum if he'd had an upset recently; perhaps his best chum had left the nursery. She couldn't think of anything so I questioned how much control he had over his life. She admitted not much, so I suggested that she introduce some more choices for him. It was as simple as that. Letting him choose which T-shirt and shorts to wear in the mornings solved the problem literally within days. **Nanny Sarah**

Once your toddler is confidently clean and dry during the daytime, you can introduce the idea of going to bed nappy-less.

Sweet Dreams

Most childcare books suggest sleep programmes for babies from the earliest age. These regimes are designed to get a baby to sleep quietly, irrespective of his wishes or fears about being left alone. Having cared for thousands of children for over a century, Norland Nannies never take this approach. Nanny prefers a bedtime routine, a set of events that you carry out in the same order every night. Nanny calls these 'sleep clues' and they go like this:

- Bath and splash time
- Warm bottle or beaker of milk
- Teeth clean
- Bedtime story
- Kiss and lights out

The same nightly routine at home or on holiday will trigger your child's body clock to start slowing down and prepare for the land of nod.

Soothing music at bedtime can also be part of your sleep clues, but do remain consistent, even on holidays or overnight visits, otherwise intermittent use of music may be seen as a treat and become interesting. Nanny knows two families who played classical music nightly but forgot the CD when they went on holiday, which caused problems as you can imagine.

Your baby will also be helped to sleep if you avoid the television and too much physical activity in the hours leading up to bed. Both will stimulate him rather than help him to wind down.

If your toddler's daytime nap is causing problems at bedtime, perhaps shorten it or bring it forward, but a daytime nap is still important for your child so do not cut it out too soon. Now that he can sit up unaided, you may be tempted to put him in front of the television while you get some household jobs done, but sleep is far more beneficial for him. A tired child becomes a 'wired' child, unlike adults who become snoozy. Lack of sleep affects behaviour and mood. An afternoon nap will help your toddler to cement everything he has learned during the morning into his brain and will help to restore his good humour. The phrase 'sleep on it' contains lots of truth, because while asleep we all consolidate what we have learned during the day, and this is most important for your toddler's developing brain. Do put him outside in his pram, lying flat, for fresh air.

Remember that your child will also require a good night's rest. Most toddlers need 10–12 hours' sleep every night. Research shows that this is still necessary even when your child reaches double figures. 'Early to bed and early to rise, makes a man healthy, wealthy and wise' – very true, but not a Nanny original!

Once you have established your bedtime routine, remember to explain it to granny, nannies and babysitters, and ask them to stick to it in your absence.

If any of my charges are difficult at bedtime, I introduce them to the 'Nanny watch', an invisible and magic timepiece given to me when I graduated from Norland. Its alarm is only audible to nannies and parents, and goes off when a child is late for bed. If they're up truly late, even they can hear it beep (it's a tune on my mobile phone alarm). It's been such a success, I always make a thing of handing the 'Nanny watch' to parents when I leave a position. **Nanny Anita**

TIME FOR A BIG BED

Your toddler will need somewhere new to sleep now that he is around two years old and has outgrown his cot. When buying a 'big boy' bed, take your child along with you. Get him to bounce on the mattresses in the shop; include him at every stage and you will probably find his excitement will carry him through any anxiety about this big change in his life. Items to buy with your new bed are:

- Good mattress but remember you will probably be replacing it once your toddler is over the wet-bed years
- Mattress protector to help with accidents
- Fitted bottom sheets or flat sheets
- Duvet and cover
- Pillow and pillowcase
- Temporary cot side to avoid falling out (optional)

When you feel it's time for a pillow and duvet, let him choose the design for his duvet cover because he is bound to have favourite story characters by now.

A temporary cot side could help with those first few weeks when falling out of bed might be an issue. This is a net stretched across a frame with two arms that tuck under the mattress to secure it. Alternatively, a flat sheet used underneath a duvet cover tucked in on both sides is a cheaper option and has the same anti-falling out effect. Nanny knows one family who still use a heavy grain-filled soft toy, good old Lavender Rabbit, placed on the outside edge of the bed, to hold down the duvet and stop their five-year-old rolling out.

NANNY'S TOP TIP

For a toddler who feels he has too much space in his new bed, use a flat sheet to 'apple pie' the bed. Tuck in the foot end higher up the bed to shorten the legroom.

Just in case all your efforts to promote a 'big boy' bed to your little one do not go according to plan, do not dismantle the cot before your toddler is happy with his new bed otherwise you may end up with no cot and a toddler refusing to go to bed.

BED-WETTING

This can cause stress for both parents and children alike. Nanny has one firm rule: bed-wetting is *never* worthy of your anger or dissatisfaction. If a toddler wets the bed, it is simply an accident; and if an older child does it, then you should be asking what has changed or what might be wrong. Give him space to talk to you and if you think there is a physical problem, speak to your doctor.

Once your toddler is out of night-time nappies, ensuring he uses the toilet before bed, and perhaps again before you turn in, will help him to stay dry through the night. If the worst happens, always stay calm and soothe your child. Change the sheets then settle him back to sleep.

BUMPS IN THE NIGHT

As his imagination develops, so will your toddler's ability to hear things that are not there. He may invent monsters under the bed or become scared of the dark. Rest assured it is a phase and it will pass. In the meantime, breathe deeply – these matters are extremely real for your child. It might help if he sees you checking under the bed and in cupboards to reassure him he is alone. Make this part of your bedtime routine until the phase passes. Bad dreams and night terrors can affect pre-schoolers and older children. His nightmare may have woken the household, but stay calm and soothe him back to sleep. It might help to discuss a nightmare the next day with an older child just in case some physical event has triggered it, like a scrap at school.

NOTE ON SLEEPWALKING

Never wake a sleepwalker. Take your child gently by the arm and lead him back to bed calmly and quietly. If he wakes, reassure him and settle him back to sleep. If sleepwalking is persistent, ensure your upstairs is safe by closing the bathroom door and using a stair gate to prevent a night-time tumble down the stairs. Try to get to the bottom of this new phase in your child's life: talk about what might have changed or might be worrying him.

First Teeth

Cutting his first tooth could turn your little angel into a grizzly toddler. You are going to have to bear with him during this difficult patch.

He will cut his bottom front teeth first, then the top front ones. When he is around a year old, his molars or back teeth will appear. By the time he is two and a half to three years old, he will have a full set of 20 milk teeth. Apart from spotting a tiny sliver of white jutting through his gums, the main symptoms of teething are:

- Pain – caused by movement in the jaw as the tooth pushes upwards
- Red cheeks and gums
- Dribbling
- Poor appetite
- Need to chew
- Raised temperature (not above 38°C when it is classed as a fever)

If your baby develops a fever or has diarrhoea, then you should seek medical advice, because this is something more than just teething.

As each tooth appears, try to alleviate the symptoms. Nanny suggests the following:

- Teething rings are plastic rings you pop in the fridge (never the freezer) to cool and give to your baby to suck and chew. Never attach it to your baby's clothing with a ribbon; this is a choking hazard.
- Carrot sticks or pieces of apple for a weaned baby are good to chew on.
- Cool drinks, but never icy, can be offered.
- Teething gels can be used for worse cases. Ask your pharmacist to advise you before you use this mild local anaesthetic. Rub it on to your baby's gums with a clean finger and always follow the instructions on the box.
- Pain relief is a last resort. Always follow the medical instructions for dosage on the box.

If a lot of dribbling is causing a rash around your baby's mouth, keep a tissue to hand to dab it dry. Alleviate any dribble rash with a neutral petroleum jelly ointment. Also administer lots of cuddles.

A Grand Day Out

As your baby becomes a learner-walker then toddler, you will be leaving your pram behind and looking for something more compact you can handle while your child takes an occasional walk. It is time to go shopping for a buggy or stroller. Nanny has a strong preference here: choose a pushchair in which the child faces the pusher. Your child's brain is developing at a rate it will never match again, so there are good reasons to opt for a parent-facing buggy. British research in 2008 ('Talk to Your Baby', Dundee/ Sutton Trust) showed that children who had away-facing buggies did not talk as early; they had slightly raised heart rates while in the buggy and did not readily sleep in it. The researchers suggested the last two observations meant the children were stressed, which was supported by observing slower heart rates of the same toddlers when placed in parent-facing buggies.

If you cannot see your child's face, neither of you is communicating. The research showed that parents and babies who faced each other smiled and laughed significantly more. This is simple communication and can progress to chatting and learning. Look for the 'Walkie Talkie' label in pushchair catalogues and in shops to help you choose a parent-facing buggy. Every pushchair, like his old pram, should have internal reins or fixing points for your own reins to keep your toddler safe and prevent him being accidentally tipped out.

While you are out and about with your toddler, remember that bus drivers, shop assistants and other adults are all there to help you – be brave enough to ask rather than struggle with shopping and a buggy, and end up snapping at your toddler. If asked directly, people will find it hard to refuse to hold doors for you or help you up steps.

Risky Business

Your child has probably been practising his new skills on his own before he shows his accomplishments to you. It may fill you with dread to learn that he has already climbed out of his cot without your knowing, that he has climbed the stairs or opened the fridge door all alone. He is testing out his world to see what it does, but his exploration does not have to be a risky business.

SAFETY IN THE HOME

When your baby starts to crawl, try getting down at his height to see what the immediate dangers might be. Remember, your baby is watching your every move, so if he sees you crawling, he may copy you. While you are both on your knees, give him a running commentary on what is out of bounds in the sitting room, then crawl through to the kitchen and talk him through the do's and don'ts of cupboards and doors. Starting this routine from the minute he is mobile will help steady your nerves without having to cover your home in foam padding.

Once he is a confident walking toddler give him the skills to live in your house the way it is, and you will probably not need stair gates or childproof locks on your kitchen cupboards for long. What Norland Nannies do is 'teach' the toddlers in their care how to cope in their homes and they make it fun – that way the toddlers do not spot an education session. A tricky staircase is easily dealt with by playing 'climbing Everest' for a day. Find a short piece of rope, pack a small rucksack with toys, juice and some biscuits and you can have great fun climbing the Himalayas until you are certain your child is confident on your stairs. If he is being self-reliant and trying to get himself a drink from the fridge, but failing to close it, then you can spend time in the kitchen together making a meal and asking him to fetch everything you need from the fridge one item at a time. Every time he finds what you have asked for, just remind him to close the fridge door behind him. Repetition of a single action should help him to keep in mind what routine he needs to fulfil when he decides to do it alone.

Risk is all part of growing up, but as parent and carer it is your duty to ensure your child is as safe as possible. Some risks require rules; others need your vigilance. So running with a lollipop in your mouth is a 'no', and older siblings playing with tiny Lego with a baby around is a 'no' that means the bigger children play in their bedroom. Nanny's safety list is by no means exhaustive, but take a read and you will begin to get the idea of what to judge as safe and what to rectify until your child is older.

Nanny's Household Safety Checklist:
- **Electric plugs and sockets** are toddler-free zones. Your toddler should know from the outset he is not allowed to switch on lamps or the television, and he must not insert plugs into sockets. Buy childproof socket covers for all the sockets in your child's bedroom and in the living rooms downstairs. This way he cannot poke his fingers or toys into the holes.
- **Trailing cables** are trip hazards for little walkers, sending table lamps and DVD decks crashing to the floor. Think about taping down any cables you cannot re-route or safely hide under carpets.
- **Heavy doors** are dangerous for small hands that always seem to find their way into the doorjamb. From now on, doors should either be properly closed behind you or held open with a suitable doorstop.
- **Window locks** are not essential, but take a judgement on how easy your windows are to open. If your child's

room has a low windowsill he can climb on, then locks might be necessary. For all upstairs windows, try not to place furniture in front of them, which might aid access to window latches. However, a child who has been trained not to climb on the armchairs in the sitting room will probably not be able to reach the latches on downstairs windows until he has grown taller.

- **The kitchen** can be a hazardous place for a toddler, but lay down some ground rules before you start to redesign your units. If a toddler knows *never* to touch the oven then he cannot be left to judge for himself when it is hot or cold. As an Aga is always hot, this advice works well. When cooking, use the rear rings on the stove rather than the front ones and always turn pan handles inwards so they cannot be reached by a stretching toddler. Keep knives in drawers high up and possibly locked. Push kettles to the back of the work surface. Fit childproof locks to kitchen drawers and cupboards; you can remove them once the inquisitive pre-school years are behind you.

- **Cleaning fluids** must be locked away. Since many households keep these items in the cupboard under the sink, this is one door that should be completely child-proof, even if all the bottles also have childproof caps.

- **Medicines and the medicine box** should be out of reach in a high cupboard, and preferably out of sight to avoid temptation for Detective Inspector Toddler. If your child is adept at manoeuvring his highchair to reach his goal, then medicines and other no-go substances should be locked away.

- **Stair gates,** especially on the landing, are essential to keep young ones safe. While you are showering, you can rest assured that your toddler can roam from his bedroom on to the landing safely. If standard stair gates do not fit your house, then make one yourself. Try not to let DI Toddler see you working the lock. It may be childproof, but he will spend hours trying to work it out, and if you give him clues he will figure it out far faster.

- **Banisters** in modern homes now comply with regulations to ensure the distance between rails is no wider than the average baby's head. Be aware that old houses may have banisters that do not comply with current regulations. This is perhaps another opportunity to instigate some Nanny wisdom on how to use the stairs and the banisters safely.

- **Street doors** should be kept firmly closed at all times to prevent toddlers pottering out into the road.

- **Fires and radiators** are no-go zones. Explain to your toddler they are hot all the time; that way he will always avoid them. A fireguard is essential to protect your toddler while he is unsteady on his feet and curious to boot.

- **Hot drinks** on coffee tables now go on higher shelves if you have to place them down. Otherwise, you might have to save hot drinks for his nap times to avoid accidents.

- **Alcoholic drinks** should be kept under lock and key.

- **Sharp corners** on furniture can be difficult to solve. If you do not want to tape foam padding to all hard edges, tuck a sharp-edged nest of tables between two armchairs so the corners are no longer at eye height for your toddler. You can pad sharp corners on dining tables and kitchen counters or fit some safety corners from a baby and toddler shop. If you are buying new furniture with a toddler around, you might be happier looking for pieces with round corners for the time being.

- **Toilet seats and lids** should be kept down. This prevents toys disappearing round the U-bend and is also more hygienic when you flush. You can get locks to keep the seat lid down if your toddler is particularly inquisitive.

- **Hot taps** are out of bounds from the very first bath your baby takes (see Chapter 1). Reinforce this rule and the reasons why every time your toddler takes a bath or washes his hands at the sink. Scalds on baby soft skin are particularly horrific.

- **Non-slip bathmats** are essential for families to avoid slipping and cracking heads on hard porcelain surfaces.

- **Gardens and sheds** pose a new range of risks for toddlers. Take a look round your garden, checking for dangerous tools left out, garden chemicals not put back on high shelves in the shed and enticing hoses still connected to the tap. Also, think about what plants you have in your garden. Foxgloves, euphorbia, hyacinths and many, many others are either poisonous or irritants, and any reaction is likely to be more serious in a toddler. If you have a toddler intent on exploring every corner of your garden, you may have to dig up the worst offending plants; otherwise a walk round the garden together pointing out what is out of bounds, and why, will start to educate your child on safety as well as horticulture. At first, you might have to take this walk daily before any outside play can begin.

- **Garden ponds** are very tempting to toddlers, so they should be covered or fenced off to prevent your child falling in.

- **Driveways and fences** should also be inspected for safety, with the constant question 'can he escape?' in mind. You might think about temporary netting across gaps in hedges, and you will certainly have to rule out the driveway as a play area.

NANNY'S TOP TIP
Do not dictate 'that is out of bounds' without offering an explanation. A blank 'no' is likely to promote exploration, but a child whose intelligence is respected will understand if you reinforce the rule and 'why' regularly.

Norland Nannies do spot-checks for safety all the time at home. A quick peek round the kitchen or garden at a friend's birthday party to see what you can spot will contribute to a happy playtime rather than one fraught with danger.

SAFETY ON THE MOVE
When you are out and about, Nanny has in-car safety guidelines, a pavement policy and rules on stranger danger.

Nanny's In-car Safety Guidelines:
- Only parents and carers open and close car doors so that little fingers are not squashed
- Only adults are responsible for buckling up child car seats
- No toys on the rear parcel shelf to avoid them flying forwards in a crash
- No playing with car seat buckles
- No distracting the driver by throwing empty beakers or similar forwards

- No children in the front seat
- No children in a seat with an airbag facing them
- No winding down windows or leaning out

NANNY'S TOP TIP

Keep your car keys in your pocket while strapping your child into his seat. A child who has managed to lock himself in while you are walking round to the driver's door may not cooperate and see your frantic attempts to unlock the car as a game.

A lot of Norland Nannies take a basic car maintenance course before they graduate to avoid being caught out with a broken down car and a small child. Most take an advanced driving course to learn to cope with icy or wet conditions. They will do whatever it takes to ensure both they and the children they care for are as safe as possible.

Nanny's Pavement Policy:

- Always hold hands with a toddler or use reins when out and about – there is no age limit here. Nanny knows one family whose five-year-old still uses reins in crowded places and alongside big city roads.
- Always keep your child on the inside of the pavement away from traffic.
- Older children can walk in front of you, but must wait at corners for you to catch up, always remaining in your line of sight.
- When crossing the road always stop on the pavement, look both ways and listen.
- Always use zebra and pelican crossings where available.
- Always wait for the green man to show on pelican

crossings because small children need to adhere to the rule and not judge for themselves if it is safe to cross.

NANNY'S TOP TIP

In car parks, erect the pushchair and get your bag out of the car before you get your child out. On your return, put him back in his car seat first, then load the shopping. This way he cannot run free in a dangerous environment.

Nanny's Stranger Danger Rules:
- Children can say good morning to strangers when accompanied by mummy or daddy, but not through the school fence. Explain why simply and avoid being scary.
- Teach your child his home address and telephone number, and check regularly that he remembers both.
- Teach your child how to spot a policeman and explain how he can help.
- Do not put your child's name on a sticker on the outside of his coat – a stranger may use it to gain your child's trust. Your toddler may think that if the stranger knows his name, then he probably knows mummy too.
- It is acceptable for your child to scream and kick if a stranger tries to pick him up.
- Coach your child to tell a police officer, someone behind the counter in a shop or someone with other children with them if he needs help or is lost.

Hopefully, your child will never experience an encounter with a stranger intent on doing him harm. As an adult, it can be hard to understand what might upset a little one, even if the stranger had the best intentions, so encourage your child to talk to you about anything that is bothering him. He may have heard that bad strangers might touch him inappropriately but not truly understand what this means, and then if he does meet a helpful stranger who puts a reassuring hand on his shoulder, this could be misconstrued. Only you know the signals that your child gives off if he is worried or withdrawn. Keep an open eye and mind for anything that might change in your child as he gets older and more independent.

NANNY'S TOP TIP

Getting lost at the shops is terrifying for children, so introduce a simple game. If lost, the child stands still and calls out at the top of his voice: 'One two three, where are you?' He continues repeatedly, shouting it out until you can home in on his beacon and scoop him up for a reassuring cuddle.

Teaching your child what is safe and what might be dangerous is a continuous occupation during his first years. Try not to issue a 'don't' without offering a 'why'. However, there are times when a sharp shout to warn him of a danger he cannot see is needed; or you may need to lift him away from a hazard to which he is continually attracted. Nanny lives in the real world – all children have accidents – so offer respect, advice and encouragement, and know when to step in to prevent accidents.

Remember, your child is picking up everything he knows from you so you too have to be perfectly behaved. Since he is now constantly mimicking mummy and daddy, perhaps it is time to use your little helper's newfound skills with cleaning the house, tidying up or learning to cook.

CHAPTER 4
nanny in the kitchen

Cooking wonderful, nutritious food for your children can be a great pleasure, but it's often a source of worry for new parents, especially for those who don't have much time to cook, or who don't like cooking. In this chapter, Nanny will give you tips and tactics for weaning and getting your children to eat healthily. She will guide you through basic kitchen hygiene, dealing with the fussy eating stage and introducing good table manners, and she will suggest fresh, tasty recipes that are quick and easy to make. More than that, this chapter will inspire you and your child to have fun in the kitchen together, making and eating tasty home-cooked food.

Kitchen Hygiene and Safety

Nanny always looks at the kitchen from a baby's point of view and asks herself what forgotten nooks and crannies might be tempting to small fingers, and what is at floor level that might not be seen? We know that cookers, kettles and plug sockets are all potential hazards (see 'Nanny's Household Safety Checklist', Chapter 3, page 99). It is also important to make sure your kitchen is 'healthy'. Babies and very young children are susceptible to tummy bugs as they haven't yet developed the immune system to cope with some of the germs that do not affect adults. Upset tummies and food poisoning can be avoided with some basic rules of kitchen cleanliness.

The kitchen floor is where your baby will be crawling, so keep it mopped and swept regularly. That piece of uncooked pasta that dropped under the table will doubtless find its way into baby's mouth if you or your dog haven't spotted it first, so you need constantly to keep an eye out for objects that have dropped into the 'baby zone'.

Nanny tends to avoid using chemical sprays for cleaning, as some medical experts link household cleaning products to an increase in childhood ailments such as asthma. Use eco products that avoid unpleasant chemicals, or some of the best old-fashioned antibacterial cleaners such as diluted white vinegar, baking soda, lemon juice or tea tree oil in solution.

NANNY'S TOP TIP FOR A 'GREEN' CLEAN

To clean sinks and tiles and scrub tables and worktops, use a paste made up of two parts bicarbonate of soda to one part vinegar or lemon juice. Add a few drops of lemon essential oil to the mix for a fresh scent. Once you have wiped down with the paste, rinse or wipe off with a clean wet cloth.

Kitchen cleanliness need not become an obsession. Your child doesn't need to be in a totally sterile environment; just one that is safe and clean. It's not possible to rid your home of all 'nasties', and Nanny knows one scientist mum (and many grandmas) who believes that a bit of dirt is a good thing, as it helps children develop a strong immune system. So use your common-sense.

Rather than spending your days scrubbing and washing every-thing, Nanny knows that the most useful tip for keeping your family healthy is to make sure they have a routine of washing hands before cooking or eating. Introduce this as soon as your baby is sitting up at the table to eat his first weaning meal. Make a game of it by singing songs (the obvious one is 'this is the way we wash our hands'); you'll find that even small children will follow basic rules of hygiene if you make it fun from the start.

Is My Baby Ready for Weaning?

With a spotlessly clean and safe kitchen, the first big food milestone for any new parent is weaning. This is when your baby moves from milk to solid food.

For the first months of life, babies only need breast or formula milk, but most are ready to start on solids when they are around six months old. If your baby was born prematurely, he may not be ready for weaning at six months, so it is always best to check with your health visitor or GP before you start your baby on solids.

Babies are born with their own supply of iron, but around six months it will begin to run low, which is one of the reasons why you need to introduce new foods. Often you will find that it is your baby who tells you, in no uncertain terms, when he is ready for something other than milk. Here's what to look out for:

Nanny's 'Ready for Weaning' Signals:
- Is he still crying for more after a feed?
- Is the time between each feed getting shorter?
- Is he waking more at night?
- Is he showing interest in what you are eating?
- Is he beginning to chew or suck anything he can get his tiny hands on?

If he is ready for weaning, Nanny recommends freshly made *home-cooked* food (preferably organic and locally grown). Before you scream, throw the book across the room and reach for the nearest supermarket jar of puréed apple – STOP! Let's be honest here: most parents are going to use off-the-shelf baby food at some point, and there is no problem with that; there are very good ready-made foods on the market. However, home-cooked food is cheaper in the long run and best for baby as you know exactly what ingredients have gone into it.

Making your own baby foods needs a little preparation and forward planning but it's simple when you know how – it's as easy as popping the lid off a jar and warming up its contents.

GETTING STARTED

Before you start making your own weaning foods, some basic kitchen equipment will help.

Nanny's Weaning Equipment Essentials:
- A **stick blender or food processor** will save time and money, but if you don't have one use a sieve and a wooden spoon.
- A **steamer** is the best way to cook vegetables and fruit; it keeps the vitamins and taste in rather than boiling it away. If you don't have one you can use a colander or sieve in a saucepan as a cheaper alternative.
- **Baby weaning spoons** that have no sharp edges.

The best way to cook baby foods is to steam, stew, boil or bake. There are a few things to avoid when preparing foods for weaning: salt and sugar should not be used because a baby's kidneys cannot cope with them, and never fry food.

Freezing Baby Foods

To save time, make puréed foods in batches to freeze in ice cube trays, ziploc bags or sterilised plastic tubs. Ice cube trays are Nanny's favourite because two cubes make an ideal baby-sized meal. Your baby will only take one or two spoonfuls of food at first and you can pop a small amount out when needed. What's great about ice cube trays is that you can cook single batches (such as potato purée and carrot purée) and then once your baby is used to taking the single flavour, you can mix and match to create mini-meals.

Weaning can sometimes appear daunting to new parents, so Nanny has set out some easy menus and recipes for the three main weaning stages. Before we look at what you can cook for your baby, you need to know how to encourage your little 'breast or bottle lover' to take food from a spoon.

Hints for Easy Weaning

The key to getting your child to take his first spoonful of food is to make sure you are both relaxed when you start. Weaning varies from child to child – some will take to solids immediately, while others will need more coaxing. He may cry at first or spit the food out; after all, he has never experienced these tastes or textures before, but Nanny has plenty of advice on how to make sure weaning goes smoothly:

Nanny's Successful Weaning Guidelines:
- Establish a meal-time schedule for the day.
- Give yourself plenty of time.
- Go at your baby's pace.
- Cover the floor with a mat – weaning is always a messy business.
- Talk to your baby while you are feeding, telling him what he is eating.
- Always throw uneaten food away; don't refreeze or store.

Once you have prepared your food, take your baby in your arms as if you were breastfeeding or giving a bottle. This will hopefully continue the association of a cuddle with being fed. Using a soft-edged spoon, gently and slowly offer him small quantities. If he is sitting up on his own, you could start to feed him in a chair but always make sure you are facing him. Don't force or rush him, and if he refuses the food, turns his head away, screams or spits it out he may be telling you he's had enough or he's not ready. Until now food has come as a continuous flow in liquid form so don't worry if he cries – your main aim is to get him used to the idea of eating from a spoon. He will of course still be getting most of his nourishment from milk.

WEANING STAGE ONE: SIX MONTHS PLUS

Foods to try: purées of apple, apricot, avocado, banana, carrot, cauliflower, courgette, leek, papaya, pear, peach, peas, plum, potato, squash, swede, sweet potato; baby rice

Start with thin purées of steamed vegetables or fruit, blended or sieved and cooled. At first, try preparing single flavours such as puréed potato or puréed carrots as this will help to isolate any dislikes or allergies your baby might have. Once you have tried a variety of single foods, you can then move on to combinations such as apple and banana, leek and potato and so on. All food should be cooked when you are starting out weaning. The only food that can be introduced raw at around six months is banana.

As your baby approaches eight months you can move on to purées of turkey, chicken and white fish. Make sure that you include some starchy foods (such as potatoes and rice), fruit, vegetables and protein in his daily diet.

NANNY'S TOP TIP

Use sweet eating apples, not cooking apples, for purées, but cook for longer to allow fibres to break down. Being sweeter than cooking apples, they do not require the addition of sugar.

As well as purées, one of the first foods you can try is baby rice. Mixed with his milk, this will give your baby the experience of a new texture rather than a change of flavour. Baby rice comes in powder form and is made up with breast or formula milk. It has a thin grainy texture and will encourage your baby to use his gums to chew.

> Try different tastes at each meal. Even if the baby doesn't like a particular food try it again a few weeks later as babies change in their likes and dislikes as they grow. One week they may not eat puréed apple and a month later their taste buds have developed and they eat it with gusto. **Nanny Emily**

As your baby grows, you should introduce different textures and thicknesses, such as thicker rice, purées and lumpy mash. Here are two of Nanny's favourite recipes:

NANNY'S CARROT AND PARSNIP PURÉE
What you need:
>   *3 medium carrots, peeled and diced*
>   *2 medium parsnips, peeled and sliced*
>   *1 potato, peeled and sliced*

How to cook:
1. Place the carrots, parsnips and potato into a saucepan, cover with water and bring to the boil. Simmer for 20 minutes or until tender.
2. Strain the vegetables and leave to cool. Purée in a blender.
3. Add some breast milk, cooking water or formula milk.

NANNY'S APPLE AND PEAR PURÉE

What you need:

1 ripe dessert apple and pear (peeled, cored and sliced)

Water or breast or formula milk

How to cook:

1. Place the fruit in a steamer for 10 minutes. Allow to cool.
2. Mash the fruit with a fork.
3. Add a little milk or water to thin it.

NANNY'S TOP TIP

To avoid confusion when weaning, try offering water in a beaker and save the bottle for your child's milk feeds.

WEANING STAGE TWO: EIGHT TO ELEVEN MONTHS

Foods to try: thicker purées and lumpy mash of meats, lentils and pulses, rice, small pasta shapes, non-sugared cereals, non-citrus fruits

By this stage, your baby is probably sitting in an upright highchair and eating three small meals a day in addition to his breast or bottle milk. He may be feeding himself and will probably have some teeth to help with chewing. You can start to introduce cheese, yoghurt and stronger flavours at around 11 months. This is your 'food opportunity' as it's probably the only chance you will have to influence your child's diet. Older babies will begin to express specific likes and dislikes and will refuse certain foods, but nutritionists have shown that the more varied tastes and textures introduced at this stage of weaning, the more open the baby will be to new foods as he gets older.

Snacks at this stage can include rusks, bread sticks or rice cakes, and your child will still only be drinking breast or formula milk and water. Meals can be minced or chopped, and as your baby's teeth emerge you can introduce finger foods such as thin carrot sticks, cucumber sticks and fingers of toast. Remember to remove the skin on all raw fruit to make chewing easy and choking less likely, and never leave him on his own when eating. Learning to chew is an important development stage, and not just for feeding as it also helps with the development of throat muscles involved with speech.

Here are two more of Nanny's favourite recipes for this stage:

CHICKEN WITH ROOT VEGETABLES

Makes 4 baby-sized servings

What you need:

1 chicken breast fillet

2 small parsnips or potatoes, peeled and chopped

1 medium carrot, sliced

Herbs (optional)

1 teaspoon vegetable stock

2 tablespoons single cream

How to cook:

1. Chop the chicken and poach or steam until cooked through.
2. Bring 300ml (½ pint) of water to the boil and add the vegetables, herbs, stock and cream.
3. After 5 minutes add the chicken and cook for a further 10 minutes or until the vegetables are soft.
4. Liquidise, purée or mash, depending on your baby's taste and stage.

And for pud:

RICE PUDDING WITH PRUNE JUICE

Makes 6 baby-sized portions

What you need:

    50g (2oz) pudding rice
    600ml (1 pint) whole milk
    15g (½ oz) butter
    25g (1oz) caster sugar
    60ml (2fl oz) prune juice

How to cook:

1. Preheat the oven to 150°C (fan oven 130°C)/ 300°F/Gas Mark 2.
2. Wash the rice and drain.
3. Place the rice, milk, butter and caster sugar in a greased ovenproof dish.
4. Cover with foil and cook for 1½–2 hours, stirring occasionally, until the rice is tender. Leave to cool.
5. Stir in the prune juice and serve warm or cold. Alternatively, serve with a teaspoon of fruit purée such as pear or apricot.

WEANING STAGE THREE: TWELVE MONTHS TO TODDLER

Foods to try: family foods, healthy snacks, full-fat milk

You are on the home straight now. From around 12 months, your baby can start to eat many of the foods that your family eats for dinner (unless he has any allergies), as long as they are not high in fat, sugar or salt. The way to do this is to set aside a portion of your meal before you add seasoning. Chop it finely and make sure there are no bones – that way you don't have to cook separate meals.

Introduce elevenses and afternoon tea if needed, as additional healthy snacks are good for an energy top-up. As he grows, and especially at toddler stage, start to introduce more fish. Two portions of oil-rich fish a week – salmon, sardine or mackerel – are recommended for children aged two and above. Ensure that your child has the right combination of foods every day.

Nanny's Checklist for Toddlers' Daily Intake:
- 4–5 servings of carbohydrate such as bread, rice, pasta, potatoes
- 2 portions of fruit
- 3 portions of vegetables
- 2 servings of lean meat, fish, eggs or meat alternative
- 2–3 servings of dairy products (yoghurt, cheese, milk)

Don't forget to offer a range of finger foods at lunch and supper. Bread sticks, rice cakes and vegetable batons all help to encourage self-feeding and familiarity with new textures.

NANNY'S TOP TIP

Chop spaghetti and tube pasta (penne) with scissors to avoid chasing it round the dish. In fact, scissors are handy for chopping any toddler meal including green beans, sausages, fish fingers and fish fillets.

Your little one will learn his eating habits from his parents and siblings, so make having a meal a relaxed occasion. You may not be having fun or feeling relaxed as your carefully prepared parsnip surprise is catapulted on to the kitchen floor, or when your baby refuses the wonderful apple and nectarine dessert you have prepared, but this is what children at this age do. Try not to show your frustration. The important thing is not to let meal times become a battle. Don't constantly wipe up or mop him with his bib – this will make him fussy about food dribbles and spills. Wait until the meal is over before you all help to clear up.

Remember, you also need to eat healthily yourself. Cook the same vegetables for yourself for lunch so that your child gets used to seeing you eating the same as him. As he gets older, if he sees you snacking on fruit and vegetables, rather than crisps and chocolate, he will want to do the same.

Fussy Eaters

Many parents get lulled into a false sense of security when their 'perfect babies' eat purées of spinach and carrots, broccoli and cabbage. However, as a baby grows, his tastes often change and you may find at some stage he will no longer eat vegetables and frequently decides that he doesn't want to eat his food at all. 'Don't like it', 'yuk' or just plain 'no' may become words that you learn to dread at meal times. With a toddler, fussy eating is often about attention; by refusing food he exerts some control over his own life and it is his first test of mummy's or daddy's authority. It's frustrating for parents, but there are some strategies that may encourage your child to eat up:

Nanny's Clean Plates Checklist:
- Don't let your child snack on sweets and chocolate.
- Try cutting back on drinks other than water and milk.
- Don't let him drink milk within an hour of the meal.
- Avoid getting angry when your child won't eat.
- Keep meal portions small and don't insist on him eating everything on his plate.
- Eat your meals as a family – seeing everyone else eat up may help.

With fussy eaters, I always avoid using pudding or ice cream as a reward. It's common for mums to say 'If you eat your cabbage you can have an ice cream', but this sends out the wrong message – that eating vegetables is unpleasant and eating sweets is nice. **Nanny Emily**

Nanny always gives praise when the right foods are eaten, and if a meal is left untouched the plate is removed without comment or fuss. Nagging will draw attention to the uneaten food and may make matters worse. Never cook an alternative meal as this sends your child the message that by refusing his food he gets to eat something he likes.

To expand the range of tastes and textures, introduce new foods on to the child's plate regularly. This must be done without comment. Your child will get used to seeing new foods on his plate and, when you feel he is ready, you can encourage him to try them.

I have a 'one taste' rule. Children have to take one bite of a new food and that's all. This way they get to try new things, and I've found that with some foods they do start to like them. **Nanny Louise**

One excellent way to encourage toddlers to eat up is to be artistic with their food. Make faces out of mash and vegetables or create a seabed picture with their dinner. Here is one of the Norland Nannies' favourites:

ROCK POOL DINNER WITH STARFISH AND SEAWEED

What you need:

    110g (4oz) potatoes, peeled and chopped
    110g (4oz) skinless cod fillets
    150ml (¼ pint) milk
    1 tablespoon chopped parsley
    Black pepper
    1 small egg, beaten
    2 tablespoons fresh breadcrumbs (put slightly stale bread into blender)
    Sunflower oil for frying

How to cook:

1. Boil the potatoes for about 10 minutes until tender, then drain and mash.
2. Place the cod fillets in a saucepan and cover with milk. Cook gently for 5 minutes until firm then drain and flake. REMOVE ALL BONES.
3. Mix together the mashed potato, cod and parsley. Season with black pepper. Shape into a starfish using your hands.
4. Dip the starfish into the egg and then the breadcrumbs.
5. Heat a tablespoon of sunflower oil in a frying pan and, when hot, cook the starfish in batches for 5–7 minutes, turning once until cooked and golden. Drain on kitchen paper.
6. Serve the starfish with steamed spinach ('seaweed') and carrots cut into rough fish shapes, or cut cooked potatoes into wedges and make them into boats with a lolly stick mast and paper sail.

IS HE EATING ENOUGH?

All parents worry at some point whether their child is eating enough, especially when he refuses food. Research has shown that if he is eating some food from each of the three food groups – carbohydrates, protein and fats – no matter how limited his tastes, he will get the nourishment he needs. So don't worry too much if your child hasn't eaten green vegetables for two days; it's not likely to be a problem and it will balance out over the week. However, if you are worried that fussy eating or lack of appetite might be affecting your child's health, then talk to your health visitor or doctor.

Vegetarian and Vegan Diets

Vegetarians get their protein from seeds, eggs, milk, pulses and beans, and many parents around the world successfully feed their children a meat-free diet. The principles of weaning are the same for vegetarians as they are for meat eaters in the first stage of weaning, but as your child grows his diet may require more planning and thought to ensure he gets the right balance of protein, fat and carbohydrates. Always opt for high-protein foods such as soya, root vegetables, lentils, avocados or rennet-free cheese. Vegetarians can be short of the essential vitamin B12, but this can be found in yeast, fortified cereals, breads and soya or rice milk, so make sure these are part of his daily diet. A vegetarian diet can be short of iron, so serve a green vegetable such as spinach or broccoli, but make sure you include a good source of vitamin C like orange juice, which is needed to help the absorption of iron.

Try to avoid prepared vegetarian foods from the supermarket; if you check the labels you will find they are very high in salt, but they can be useful occasionally, such as for parties and barbecues. Try simple home-made foods such as lentil and spinach purée, rice and red lentils, home-made baked beans and vegetable couscous. Always ask your health visitor for advice if you are unsure how to feed your child, or for further help there are many vegetarian cookbooks, which will give you ideas for delicious recipes for your children.

Food for a Sick and Convalescing Child

If your little one has a temperature, sore throat or cold, he may not want to eat. The best thing is not to force him, but you can provide nourishing drinks, such as a thin fruit smoothie or milk shake. Milk may make your child feel worse if he has a blocked or runny nose, but warm milk is often a good comforting drink if he wants it. With a high temperature comes dehydration, so if he is not eating make sure that he drinks water. Some children refuse even water when they are sick so to encourage him to drink, you could freeze water in ice lolly moulds for him to suck, or use multi-coloured straws or beakers to make it more interesting. Diluted fresh juice or coconut water might also tempt him to drink, but not if he has diarrhoea.

Nanny knows that a thin chicken or vegetable broth has been a nursery staple for decades for a child with a small and recovering appetite. Here's a recipe for a thin chicken soup perfect for your patient:

CLEAR CHICKEN SOUP
What you need:
   110g (4oz) boneless chicken (approx. 1 chicken breast), chopped
   1 small potato, peeled and chopped
   4–5 cups water or stock
   1 clove garlic, chopped
   1 teaspoon grated ginger
   Pepper to taste (salt if the child is over 5)

How to cook:

1. Place all the ingredients in a pan and bring to the boil.
2. Boil for 10 minutes, then simmer for a further 20 minutes.
3. Sieve or strain the liquid and serve as a clear soup.

Food Allergies

Children can inherit food allergies or develop them as they grow. When cooking for young children, you should always be aware of potential allergic reactions, especially when you are trying new foods with your baby. If, after eating, your child vomits, develops diarrhoea, has swelling of the mouth or throat or a rash, he may have an allergy (see Chapter 5 for more information on how to spot and deal with allergic reactions). To help prevent problems, Nanny always introduces any new food to a baby at lunchtime, and only one new food at a time. This means that if there is an allergic reaction to any of the ingredients, it happens in the daytime when you can identify the cause and, if necessary, get to the doctor's easily.

Some common foods can cause allergic reactions. These should be avoided in the first 12 months during weaning:

- Cows' milk and dairy produce (except formula milk, although cows' milk in a pudding is fine)
- Shellfish
- Eggs
- Nuts (not before five years old)
- Gluten, found in the outer layer of wheat, rye, barley and oats
- Strawberries
- Honey (not before two years old)
- Tahini (paste made from sesame seeds and a core ingredient of hummus)
- Citrus fruits

Although genuine food intolerances are rare, speak to your local health practitioner if you suspect your child has any allergy that might affect their diet. Some children are allergic to food additives and colourings (see below).

FOOD ADDITIVES

Where possible, try to avoid giving your child food that contains additives and chemicals. E numbers are often a problem – they may have an adverse effect on the behaviour of young children and can cause allergies. Although many of them have been banned, there are still thousands of food additives. By law, manufacturers have to list them on packaging.

E NUMBERS TO WATCH OUT FOR:

Sunset yellow (E110): found in some brands of orange squash, lemon curd and sweets. This can cause hyperactivity, mood swings, temper tantrums and poor concentration in some children.

Allura red (E129), Carmoisine (E122), Ponceau 4R (E124), Quinoline yellow (E104), Sodium Benzoate (E211): found in many sweets, drinks and cakes aimed at children. These may increase hyperactivity.

E123, E102, E124: found in some brands of orange jelly, packaged cake mix and ice cream. They can cause allergic reactions in some children.

Not all E numbers are bad but it's best to reduce additives in your child's diet. Use fresh foods as much as you can and always check labels. Nanny knows it's difficult when your child is demanding rainbow coloured pick-and-mix, but it might be worth getting them used to home-made 'sweets'. Making these together will guarantee you know what has gone into the mix. They do contain sugar, but for older children sugar has its place as an energy booster and a treat – as long as they clean their teeth afterwards.

NANNY'S TOP TIP

To avoid tooth decay, not only clean teeth twice daily, but avoid sticky sweets at tea time. Any sweets given as a teatime pudding should be chocolate – it melts easily in the mouth and leaves no sticky lumps in the gaps between teeth.

Here are Nanny's sweet suggestions for children aged over three years:

PEPPERMINT CREAMS

What you need:
>   *500g (1lb) icing sugar*
>   *4 tablespoons condensed milk*
>   *Peppermint essence (optional)*
>   *Chocolate, for dipping (optional)*

How to make:
1. Sift the icing sugar into a bowl.
2. Stir in the condensed milk.
3. Add 2 drops of peppermint essence and knead the mixture into a ball (leave this out if your child does not like peppermint).
4. Place the ball of icing on to a board dusted with icing sugar and roll out.
5. Cut out tiny shapes with a pastry cutter (star shapes or small circles are good).

6. Dip one half of each shape in melted chocolate, if you like.
7. Leave to set in the fridge.

CHOCOLATE TRUFFLES/CHOCOLATE MICE

What you need:
   175g (6oz) plain chocolate
   1 egg yolk
   25g (1oz) butter
   1 tablespoon cocoa or chocolate hundreds and thousands
How to make:
1. Melt the chocolate in a bowl over a pan of hot water.
2. Stir in the egg yolk and butter and leave in a cool place for 30 minutes until set.
3. Mould into small balls with the fingers and roll in cocoa or chocolate hundreds and thousands.
4. Put into small paper sweet cases.

For more fun with your child, make double the recipe and shape into chocolate mice by making an oval shape. Your child can transform them into mice by adding two raisins for ears, liquorice for a tail and two dots of icing for eyes.

So does Nanny allow any bought sweets? Yes, of course as a treat, but not for children under two. If you don't encourage eating sweets when your children are very young, you will find that they may be less inclined to snack on them when they are older – and think of the good that will do for their teeth.

Healthy Snacks and Lunch Boxes

Healthy snacks and lunch boxes for nursery school or day trips are essential for older children, as they burn up energy quickly racing around the park or playground. Nanny would always recommend avoiding shop-bought snacks and preparing your own.

Nanny's Checklist for Healthy Snacks:
- Raw vegetable slices
- Grapes – always seedless and sliced in two for younger children
- Rice cakes
- Bread sticks
- Marmite sandwiches (or another filling they like) on wholemeal bread
- Chopped-up fruit
- Dried fruit – apricots, apples, figs

A packed lunch should provide one-third of your child's daily requirements of protein, complex carbohydrates and calcium. Always include something tasty from each food group:

- **Protein – keeps your child alert**: Sandwiches or salads should include protein such as chicken, egg, ham, tuna or cheese.
- **Complex carbohydrates – give your child slow-release energy**: Use wholemeal bread, oats, pasta, banana or rice. Pasta or rice salads make a nice change from sandwiches.
- **Calcium – for strong bones and teeth**: For children under five use calcium-rich, whole-milk products such as cheese, yoghurt, fromage frais, yoghurt drinks, smoothies and milk shakes.
- **Don't forget the five-a-day rule – for vitamins and minerals**: Make fruit tempting by cutting some into a fruit salad in a plastic tub or include dried fruit – dried apricots are rich in vitamins and minerals.

Always involve the children in the choice and preparation of lunch boxes; they are more likely to eat their lunch if they have been part of it. Nanny also tries to make a lunch box fun, which means that older children are less likely to swap with a friend and end up with sugary or salty junk food.

> I always make a special effort with lunch boxes. I might put sandwiches in a hand-decorated paper bag or add a surprise treat, or I'll draw a smiley face on a hard-boiled egg. They really look forward to their lunches as they never know what to expect. **Nanny Emily**

Baking Days

Fifty years ago, Norland Nannies would have baking days, getting cakes and sweets ready for the week ahead. Twenty-first century life rarely allows time, but on a quiet or rainy afternoon, Nanny always takes the opportunity to bake with the children. They love to cook if you encourage them and it's wonderfully educational: reading recipes helps with their language and literacy; weighing and measuring ingredients helps them understand numeracy; and you can both get really artistic decorating biscuits and cakes.

Here are some wonderful recipes from Norland College's kitchen guru, Alison Tucker. Nanny has selected these as they are perfect for cooking with children from three years old and upwards.

GINGERBREAD MEN
What you need:
>   *175g (6oz) plain flour*
>   *2 teaspoons ground ginger*
>   *1 teaspoon bicarbonate of soda*
>   *50g (2oz) butter or margarine*

75g (3oz) soft brown sugar
2 level tablespoons golden syrup
1 egg, beaten
Icing (ready-made in tubes is often easiest for little hands)
Coloured decorations (raisins, choc drops)
A shaped cutter – available from hardware shops

How to cook:

1. Preheat the oven to 180°C (fan oven 160°C)/ 350°F/Gas Mark 4. Lightly grease a baking sheet.
2. Sift the flour, ginger and bicarbonate of soda into a large mixing bowl.
3. Add the butter or margarine and rub into the flour until the mixture looks like breadcrumbs.
4. Mix in the sugar.
5. Warm the syrup in a small saucepan until runny, then add to the flour mix with the beaten egg.
6. Mix to form a soft dough and knead until smooth. If the dough is too sticky, add some extra flour and leave to cool.
7. Roll out the dough on a lightly floured work surface. Use a cutter to make gingerbread people and place on a tray.
8. Cook for approximately 10 minutes until crisp and golden. Allow to cool.
9. Pipe icing to make hair, face and buttons – ask your child to add choc drops or raisins as decorations.

No children's cookery chapter would be complete without the perfect fairy or cup cake recipe. This is ideal for children because it is simple and fun. Your child will love putting the mixture in the cake cases and decorating them. The nice thing about this recipe is that once you have made it a few times, you don't even need the recipe: just remember the ingredients as 4: 4: 4: 2 (four ounces each of flour, sugar and soft margarine and two eggs).

FAIRY CAKES

Makes about 12 cakes

What you need:

> 110g (4oz) soft margarine
> 110g (4oz) self-raising flour, sieved
> 110g (4oz) caster sugar
> 2 eggs
> Paper baking cases

How to cook:

1. Preheat the oven to 180°C (fan oven 160°C)/ 350°F/Gas Mark 4.
2. Put all the ingredients into a mixing bowl and beat with a wooden spoon until creamy.
3. Place a spoonful of the mixture into a paper cake case.
4. Bake for about 10–15 minutes or until springy when touched. Allow to cool on a cake rack.

You can vary the recipe by replacing 25g (1oz) of flour with the same amount of cocoa for chocolate cakes, or add raisins or chocolate chips to the mix.

And to decorate ...

Mix 110g (4oz) of icing sugar and a few teaspoons of water and spread it on the buns. Decorate with sprinkles, chocolate buttons or any small sweets your children like to eat. They will love decorating – and eating the decorations.

TWINKLE TWINKLE BISCUITS

What you need:

> 65g (2½ oz) soft brown sugar
> 65g (2½ oz) soft margarine
> 1 small egg, beaten
> 150g (5oz) plain flour

1 teaspoon mixed spice
Star cake cutter
Ribbon
Sugar icing and silver cake decorations

How to cook:

1. Preheat the oven to 180°C (fan oven 160°C)/ 350°F/Gas Mark 4.
2. Mix the sugar and margarine with half the beaten egg.
3. Sift the flour and spice and mix.
4. Knead the mixture to make a firm dough.
5. Roll out so that it is 5mm thick and cut out star shapes.
6. Bake the stars on the middle shelf for 10 minutes.
7. Make a hole in one point of the star, not too near the edge, before the biscuits cool.
8. Once the biscuits are hard, thread ribbon through the holes to hang them on the Christmas tree.
9. Decorate with sugar icing and silver cake decorations.

Table Manners

Yes, it feels like something granny might have said, but teaching table manners is essential. Chapter 3 set out the basics, but mummy and daddy may need to brush up on their table manners too. There are some good common-sense rules that will ensure that meal times will be more enjoyable for everyone.

Nanny's Good Table Manners Reminders:

- Always sit up nicely.
- Use cutlery properly.
- If you are using napkins, place them on your lap. Only toddlers should tuck them into their collar.
- Wait for everyone to be served before you start eating (older children only).

- Don't talk when chewing.
- Don't eat with your mouth open.
- Don't bolt your food.
- No toys on the table when eating.
- No elbows.
- No reaching across the table for dishes.
- Place your knife and fork together on the plate when finished.
- Say please, thank you and ask to leave the table when you have finished eating.

Nanny knows that even the smallest children can be taught good manners. There will be no embarrassing moments when you are invited around to someone else's house for dinner or when you visit a restaurant.

Family Meal Times

I have a saying that 'the family that eats together, stays together'. Family meal time is really important as it is often the only time in the day when you can all sit and talk together.
Nanny Maria

It's tough for a busy working family to find time to all sit down together for meals, but Nanny recommends that you try to plan family eating as much as you can. Why? Because this is family bonding time, and if your three-year-old sees daddy eating his cabbage and holding his knife and fork correctly, then he is more likely to eat properly as well.

Not all working parents can have their evening meal at 5.30pm with the children – if not, try and make weekends a special time to eat together. Family meals are an excellent opportunity to encourage your children to develop good social skills, so make sure you discuss the news of the day and what's happening at school, including all the family in the conversation. Nanny's number one rule is: absolutely no television on in the background.

And one last little morsel ...

Nanny used to say 'an apple a day keeps the doctor away' – now of course she knows it's at least five servings of fruit or vegetable! Sometimes, though, even the healthiest home-cooked, nutritious fare isn't enough to prevent your child from catching coughs, sneezes and other ailments. Rest assured, when your little one is under the weather, Nanny will be there to hold your hand in an emergency.

CHAPTER 5
nanny to the rescue

Since the days when anaesthetic was new to medical science, Norland Nannies have been looking after sick children at home, in hospitals, and in schools and nurseries. Let's be clear, though: despite a history of being called 'Norland Nurses', they are not trained medical professionals. This chapter is not an exhaustive list of childhood diseases – you can get that elsewhere – but it explains what Nanny has learned over the years. Always remember that where Nanny's common-sense help and first aid stops, the medical professionals can be relied on to take over.

Here Nanny's knowledge is divided into four sections:

- **Practical guide to medical emergencies and routine visits** – to help you cope with a sick or injured child; everything from how to tell if your child is unwell, to taking a temperature and giving medicine, to what to grab if the school rings to tell you they are taking your child to the local emergency department. It also contains information on infant resuscitation that every parent should know.
- **Practical guide to childhood ailments and diseases** – how to recognise and treat them.
- **Practical guide to childhood accidents** – the inevitable tumbles and the more avoidable serious injuries.
- **Common infestations** – worms and lice are not very nice.

Read this chapter at leisure so you are prepared for the times when you will have to dip into it to get immediate know-how.

NOTE ON PARACETAMOL AND IBUPROFEN

Never give these medicines to an infant under three months (unless advised by a medical professional and following their strict instructions). If you use either of these, or similar medicines, as pain or fever relief for an older baby or child, you should always follow the instructions and dosage on the box. If in doubt, always consult a medical professional when dealing with sick babies and children.

Practical Guide to Medical Emergencies and Routine Visits

Nanny's good plain advice starts with common-sense medical basics:

- Trust your instincts – you know when your child is not himself.
- Keep calm in any medical emergency.
- Know when it is time to seek medical help.

HOW TO SPOT A HEALTHY CHILD

Children, particularly tiny babies, cannot tell you if they are under the weather or hurt, so a healthy child looks like this:

- Clear glowing complexion
- Shiny hair

- Dry nose
- Laughing and smiling
- Bouncing with energy
- Good appetite
- Sleeps soundly

This is the benchmark for a happy healthy child, and any deviation could indicate sickness, injury or some form of emotional upset. If you notice any change in your child's general wellbeing, it is absolutely essential you investigate further.

SIGNS OF ILLNESS

An off-colour baby can become a sick baby very quickly. He is totally reliant on you to react quickly and seek medical help. A toddler can be playful one minute and a feverish sobbing bundle the next. However, your toddler will give you subtle indicators he is brewing something if you know what to look for.

Nanny's Early Warning Illness Checklist:
- Is your child extra tired despite a good night's rest?
- Is your child lethargic and not willing to play?
- Is your child quiet or withdrawn?
- Is your child off his food?
- Is your child refusing drinks?
- Does your child feel warmer than usual?

The one reliable indicator for impending illness is a raised temperature. Children are less able to regulate their body temperature than adults, so a slightly raised temperature in a toddler can quickly become a serious temperature if not checked and the source of the problem treated.

Using a Thermometer

There are three main types of thermometer for domestic or nursery use: the old-fashioned mercury thermometer; a digital thermometer for use under the tongue or arm; and the digital ear thermometer. The last is Nanny's preferred choice because it is the most accurate and is used in hospitals, but they are expensive. Mercury thermometers are not safe for children to use under the tongue and are being phased out; most families use a digital thermometer.

NANNY FACT

A normal body temperature is 36.5°–37.2°C (97.7°–99°F). Anything over 38°C (100.4°F) is a fever.

Taking a temperature under the arm is not the most reliable method, but it is the best way for a baby or small child. Place your little one on your lap with his back against your chest. Pop the thermometer under the arm in direct contact with the skin, so ensure a vest or T-shirt is not in the way. Hold your child's arm gently against his side and wait for the thermometer to bleep, which usually takes three to five minutes. Because an underarm temperature is not accurate, adding 0.5°C to the thermometer reading will get you closer. If your older child has just eaten or drunk anything hot or cold, wait 10 minutes before you take an oral temperature. A sick toddler may not like having his temperature taken, so try distraction to keep him still – finger puppets, a picture book or story – anything to get a clear and accurate reading.

SPOTTING EMERGENCIES

This is how to recognise the symptoms that signal an imminent emergency.

Nanny's Emergency Signals:

- Is your child convulsing? Limbs twitching or jerking?
- Is your child hot (39°C or over) and moaning? Does he have a rash or spots (possibly purple) anywhere on his body that do not blanch, or disappear, if pressed?
- Is your child pale or blue and floppy?
- Is his breathing laboured, rapid or shallow?
- Is he drowsy, hard to wake up or confused?
- Does he have a raised temperature with clammy hands and feet?

Any of the above symptoms indicates that you should urgently contact your doctor or call the emergency services.

Infant Resuscitation

Every Norland Nanny hopes she will never have to use her resuscitation skills on any of her charges, but she is trained just in case of emergency. It is advisable for all parents and carers to have some infant and paediatric first aid instruction – knowledge to be learned, stored away and hopefully never used.

Calling Emergency Services for an Infant:

- Check to see if it is safe to approach your child – you cannot afford to injure yourself if you intend to help him.
- Spend only 10 seconds checking for signs of life.
- Check to see if your child is breathing – listen with your ear to his mouth and check for chest movements showing that he is breathing.

- Call his name and shout to provoke a reaction.
- Do not shake to rouse him if you think he might have been injured, particularly his neck. A gentle shake is recommended only if you know the circumstances of his injury.
- Check for a pulse by pressing your index and middle finger together against the bone on the inside of his upper arm.
- If it is safe to move him, pick him up and take him to a telephone.
- Dial emergency services.
- Shout for help from neighbours.

Once you know that help is on its way, you can begin to resuscitate a baby who is not breathing.

Resuscitation for Infants under One Year:
- Place your baby on his back on a firm surface or cradle him across the length of your forearm.
- Look in his mouth for any obstruction or foreign object.
- Keep your baby's head in line with his chest and not tilted.
- Gently support his chin with the tips of your fingers.
- Seal your lips around his mouth *and* nose. (If you cannot seal both, then choose one. If it is the nose, ensure his lips are closed to avoid air escaping.)
- Give five gentle rescue breaths over 1–1.5 seconds.
- Check to see if the chest rises and falls.
- Repeat this sequence five times.
- Check for signs of life for 10 seconds only, and if your baby is not breathing, start chest compressions.
- Place your index and middle finger midway between your baby's nipples – this is the spot for you to compress.

- Press gently, about a third of the depth of your baby's chest, at a rate of 100 compressions per minute – singing 'Nellie the Elephant packed her trunk and trundled off to the circus' will give you the right rhythm.
- After 30 compressions, give 2 rescue breaths.
- Continue with 30 compressions for every 2 rescue breaths until help arrives.

Just because you can hear the ambulance sirens, you must not stop giving resuscitation. Keep going until a paramedic tells you to stop.

Resuscitation of children over a year old and adults does not vary much, but here are the differences:

Resuscitation for Children over One Year:
- If safe to approach, give 2 rescue breaths and 30 chest compressions before you leave an older child to telephone for emergency help.
- An older child should be laid on their back on a firm surface with their head tilted gently back, one hand on the forehead, one hand supporting the chin.
- Rescue breaths are given only via the mouth with your hand gently closing the nose to avoid air escaping.
- Chest compressions are given with the palms of both hands.
- The point of chest compression is a finger's width above the point where the lower ribs meet in the centre, on the breast bone.
- Do not compress the ribs.

Choking is the main cause of emergencies in small children. See page 171 later in this chapter for how to deal with choking.

SHOCK

Hopefully, infant resuscitation will never be necessary in your home, but you may observe the effects of shock in your child after what may seem a relatively minor accident. Shock can occur after a serious accident or trauma and sometimes during a dangerous illness. The signs of shock are:

- Cold clammy skin
- Shivering
- Fast shallow breathing
- Yawning or sighing
- Rapid and weak pulse
- Looking wiped out
- Unconsciousness if severe

If your child shows any of these signs after an accident, then help him by doing the following:

- Lay your child down and raise his legs above the level of his heart if his injury will allow it.
- Place a light blanket over him to keep him warm, but not hot.
- Check his breathing and pulse frequently.
- Do not give anything to eat or drink.
- Call for emergency help.
- Stay with your child while you wait for help to arrive.

THE RECOVERY POSITION

You also need to know how to put a child into the recovery position. This is used if your child is unconscious and still breathing. It will maintain his airway and allow vomit to trickle out safely while you call the emergency services.

Roll him on to his side supported by one leg with one arm placed at a right angle to his body. Now tilt his head gently back to open his airway and place his head with one cheek to the ground to allow any fluids to flow out. Monitor his condition constantly until help arrives.

Infants under one year old are treated differently. Hold your baby in your arms and, with his mouth facing away from you, tilt his head downwards to allow vomit to exit freely. Keep him in this position until the paramedics arrive.

Now go and book yourself on to a first aid course to get practical training!

CONTACTING YOUR SURGERY

Lots of first-time parents seek their doctor's advice regularly. Many seemingly scary things can happen in those first months, which will send you dashing to the surgery. It is better to be safe than sorry and your doctor will be happy to help and advise you. However, you can make his job easier if you have some essential information to hand when you first contact him.

Nanny's 'Doctor Needs to Know' Checklist:
- Your child's age
- Your child's temperature and any discernible fever pattern
- Your child's visible symptoms – rash, vomiting, diarrhoea, injury
- Your child's overall state – breathing problems, lethargic or sleepy, any loss of consciousness, loss of appetite or desire for drinks
- Your child's address

From this information, your doctor or surgery nurse practitioner will be able to make an immediate assessment to decide whether you need emergency assistance or if you should come in for an appointment. Even if the symptoms appear minor, your doctor is likely to want to see a tiny baby because a diagnosis is hard to offer over the telephone and illness can progress very quickly in babies. It is probably just a precaution, but start to get yourself organised with a few essentials for your trip to the surgery.

Nanny's 'Visiting the Doctor' Bag:
- Spare nappies or pants
- Muslin or tea towel to mop up sick, dribble or tears
- List of any medication your child is taking
- Fever record
- Drink beaker or bottle of milk in case of a long wait
- 'The Red Book', your child's immunisation and growth record book in which you can keep any medical correspondence too

If your baby is vomiting or has an injury, you should not give him anything to eat or drink until your doctor has given you the go-ahead. Should he need an operation, he might have to wait for his digestive system to empty before he can be given an anaesthetic.

Taking a tiny baby to the doctor's is relatively simple – offer reassurance and cuddles since he may sense the change in his surroundings or your mood. However, the situation can be very different with a scared toddler or child in pain. Explain clearly everything that is happening: why you are going; how long it might take; what the doctor is likely to do; and answer any questions he might ask. This may sound impossible as you dash around the house getting ready to leave – so don't appear panicked. Make a mental note to keep your voice steady and encourage rather than instruct. You do not want a scared, rigid toddler who is impossible to strap into his car seat. Try to take a neighbour or friend with you if you are alone: one to drive and one to sit in the back of the car with your child for company.

CARING FOR A SICK CHILD

When a child is unwell, try to stick to your usual routine, but know when to give in and let him eat what he likes or sleep when he wants. A sick baby should be with you at all times, and a sick child will probably feel happier if he is downstairs tucked up on the sofa.

Spend time playing simple games on a side table like cards or do small jigsaws. A set of farmyard animals on your child's blanket makes a field; now he can drive toy tractors up and down the folds ploughing. Use your imagination, and when that runs out, ask a neighbour if they can pop to the shops for fresh art materials, glitter and new pencils to perk up your invalid. A sick child may only have the energy to listen to stories, so cuddle up with a stack of books and start reading.

When it comes to feeding a sick child, gone are the days of 'feed a cold and starve a fever'. Lots of drinks and fresh food are best, but occasional treats to stimulate a poor appetite will do no harm. As long as fluids are being taken, a young child can manage for a couple of days without a proper meal. He will eat again when he is ready. However, if complete lack of appetite continues for more than three days, seek medical advice. If an unweaned baby has been refusing fluids (his only source of nutrition and hydration) for more than eight hours, get to a doctor immediately.

A child who has had a tummy upset might prefer light meals, or snacks like dry toast, to start with after the vomiting has stopped. See Chapter 4 for ideas on thin soups and foods to entice your patient.

It is rotten luck, but a fact of life, that as the carer of a sick child you will most probably catch whatever he has, but no self-respecting Norland Nanny would leave a family unprepared if she fell sick too. While your patient is resting, take the opportunity to cook a few 'pot meals' like stews or pies, anything that can be easily heated up for the rest of the family when you take to your bed. Prime a relative or neighbour so they are ready to help with the school run and shopping if you succumb.

TAKING MEDICINE

A spoonful of sugar may have helped the medicine go down for Mary Poppins, but not nowadays. With a tiny baby, your only difficulty in administering medicine will be in getting him to accept it without spitting out this strange taste. When he is older, convincing him that his medicine is necessary may be a little harder.

Medicine for a Young Baby

Babies up to around 18 months should be offered medicine in suspension (liquid) form. Give this to your baby with a no-needle dosing syringe or dropper. Always follow the dosage instructions supplied with the medicine and, if necessary, ask the prescribing pharmacist for advice on time intervals between doses. Most pharmacists offer a syringe and bottle-stopper kit with medicines for young babies. Remember, if your baby is under a year old, you will need to sterilise the syringe and stopper before use. Once perfectly sterile, you can fit the bottle stopper and syringe together to draw up the correct amount of medicine.

Sit down, and with your baby cradled in the elbow of one arm, pop the syringe into the side of your baby's cheek, then gently and slowly depress the syringe, giving your baby time to swallow. To help a tiny baby accept all of his medicine, it is a good idea to give a small amount, withdraw the syringe and wait before slipping it into his mouth again. A muslin square or piece of kitchen towel to hand will mop up any dribbles. Take it carefully because your baby needs a full dose for the medicine to work.

Medicine for an Older Baby

Try giving an older baby his medicine while he is sitting up in a high chair. Continue to use a syringe to give medicine because one sip of this strange taste and he may well knock a spoon out of your hand in protest.

Nanny does not recommend hoodwinking a child into taking medicine, so try to explain why he is taking medicine and gain his cooperation. Involve him by asking if he would like it on a spoon or syringe. Obviously, he must not handle his medicines, but you might win him over if you ask him to watch you pouring it out and tell you when you have reached the correct mark. Have a couple of slices of fresh fruit or his favourite juice available immediately after his medicine to take away any horrid flavour.

Medicine for Toddlers and Older Children

This may be liquid or tablet form. If an older child is prescribed tablets, ask your doctor if these are suitable to be dissolved in water or juice. Not all medicines can be taken in a dissolved form, but this is the best way to help a child to swallow tablets.

Always remember to return unused medicines to the pharmacist for proper disposal.

EMERGENCIES AT SCHOOL

Once your child is at school, you hand over responsibility for his medical care as well as his education during school hours. Nanny has received her share of calls from the headteacher asking her to attend the local emergency department because her charge has had an accident. Over the years, Nanny has learned to stay calm, leave quickly and grab the following as she heads out the door:

Nanny's Emergency Grab and Go Essentials:
- Mobile phone
- Useful phone numbers
- Money – change for drinks, sandwiches, phone calls
- Child's toothbrush and toothpaste
- Child's favourite cuddly toy or comfort blanket
- Child's book or comic

If your child has to stay in hospital overnight, the nurses will provide pyjamas and some toys, but if you have all of the above on you, then you are properly equipped to organise the collection of your other children and rally the help of your partner or neighbours. Everything else – like his favourite PJs, somewhere for you to sleep or getting a meal – can be sorted out once you are by his side.

EMERGENCIES INVOLVING YOU

You know how to dial for emergency help, but you should also be prepared for the possibility that it might be you who is hurt. In this eventuality, having spent some time practising 'calling an ambulance for Teddy' to teach your child the crucial steps to dialling the emergency services may save your life. Remember to ensure he understands that dialling the emergency services is never a game. Ambulance control centres are trained to help toddlers who are brave enough to pick up the phone. They will coax out of him the essential details if the worst happens and keep him talking long enough for them to be able to trace the call, but you need to have trained your toddler to do his bit first.

GOING INTO HOSPITAL

No one likes visiting the doctor, but for small children medical visits can be particularly distressing. If your child has to pay a visit to the hospital, getting him there with minimal fuss or upset depends on how well you 'market' this new experience to him. Nanny relies on being truthful, supportive and always by her patient's side.

A planned hospital visit can mean a procedure or operation, or a condition that needs frequent medical help. If this is the case, your child is probably already in discomfort and a little scared. Explain why the doctors need him to stay in hospital and what is going to happen. Be truthful about pain or stitches or any other medical interventions your doctor has discussed. Fear of the unknown, coupled with a colourful imagination, can cause terrible upset. During consultations, keep your child in the room with you if he wants to stay after the doctor has examined him. He should hear everything the doctor is describing and then he can ask questions of both of you. It is his body you are discussing so help him to feel included.

In the interval between consultation and actual hospital stay, prepare your toddler further by playing 'Teddy goes to hospital', or look at suitable medical books with an older child. The more he knows about what is going to happen, and when, the better. Some hospitals offer 'pre-hospital stay and play days' for your child to meet the nurses, see the ward and become generally familiar with the hospital environment. This can reap huge benefits for the success of the actual stay and your child's peace of mind.

Only you know how anxious your child can become, so plan how near to a hospital visit you start the countdown. Do not give too much notice, but do not make it a complete surprise. Mentioning 'three sleeps to go before we see the nurses' three nights beforehand may help, as may a chat about what his hospital bed and toys might be like. Your child might find solace in planning for himself by writing a list of all the personal items he wants to take with him. With a toddler you could spend time in the bedroom choosing his favourite PJs, teddy and books, and putting them in his hospital bag together.

NANNY'S TOP TIP

Write or sew your child's name on everything he takes into hospital. If his PJs end up in the hospital laundry or he swaps books with his bed-neighbour, you can find everything on discharge.

Your patient will feel happier if you can stay with him. Many children's wards offer overnight accommodation to parents, especially for long-stay patients. Ask about these facilities in advance.

Children's wards have play therapists, but they are thinly spread so try to stay as long as you can during the day to help occupy your child. Make sure you are with him when the doctors are examining him – he will need your support to give him the confidence to ask questions.

Some children become more babyish when they go into hospital. It is hardly surprising that this scary experience makes them regress. If you notice this, then do discuss it with the nurses so they can offer greater comfort and be part of your child's inner circle too.

Your child may not be allowed out of bed to play so choose games that can be classed as 'blanket top' entertainment. Magnetic jigsaws you can do in the box are ideal, as are drawing paper and pencils (not pens for fear of drawing on matron's bedding) or a small box of Lego with a tray to keep all the pieces together. Story and picture books are an age-old winner.

Be prepared for a hint of disappointment when your child is discharged. Many children adapt very quickly to life in hospital, making friends among the nurses and other patients. Going home can be a wrench, so plan for this too. You might discuss what your child would like for his first dinner home. You could buy him a small new toy as a reward for being such a brave trooper, or have his teddies lined up on the stairs as his welcoming committee. Make it fun and entertaining, and take those first days at home easy.

GOING TO THE DENTIST

The dentist can be very daunting since regular visits normally start at around five years old, at which point your child is all-seeing, knowing and questioning. If your past tactics have been to fool him into doing something he might not like, that is going to have to stop. Full disclosure is the only way forward. A recce to the dentist is a good idea. Take him along a couple of times when you visit so he gets used to the environment and instruments; ask if he can have a ride in the dentist's chair. If the dental surgery does not appear a strange and scary place, then your battle is half won. Total victory comes by choosing a child-friendly dentist, someone fun who comes personally recommended. A child who understands why he should keep his teeth spotlessly clean and visit the dentist regularly is a child who will hopefully avoid ever having a filling.

Practical Guide to Childhood Ailments and Diseases

Now that you know how to deal with emergency situations and have some basic first aid skills, Nanny will run through all the childhood illnesses and ailments she has experienced. Here are Nanny's most encountered offenders, how to spot them and what to do about them.

PROBLEMS IN YOUNG BABIES

Tiny babies are susceptible to lots of illnesses simply because they have yet to build up a personal immunity against infection. In those first months, you can expect a number of ear infections and chest infections as your baby's immune system slowly develops the ability to fight off bacteria that he will quite happily obliterate in a year's time.

Chest Infections

These are hard to detect in young babies. Your baby might have a cough because mucus from a cold is running down the back of his throat. If he is feeding properly and you cannot hear a wheeze, offer him a drink to alleviate a dry tickle, or he might be more comfortable if propped or sat up. However, a cough with a temperature, wheeze, breathlessness or loss of appetite might lead you to suspect an infection, in which case seek a doctor's help. If you suspect croup (see page 157) in a small baby, see your doctor promptly.

Ear Infections

These can be particularly nasty for your baby and you alike. The first signs of earache are a grisly mood, frequent crying and tugging or rubbing of the offending ear. He might have a raised temperature too. Always consult a doctor about treatment for a newborn baby. It is best to seek help before sleepless nights and an upset baby end in a fractious carer.

FEVER

Your child has a fever if the thermometer reads 38°C or above. There are several steps to take before contacting your doctor, unless of course you can see your child is obviously seriously ill:

Nanny's Fever Do's and Don'ts:
- Do remove outer clothing and strip your child to his vest and pants or nappy to reduce temperature.
- Do not put him to bed in pyjamas and do not tuck him in tightly because he must be able to kick off his bedclothes if he gets too hot.
- Do keep your child in a ventilated, but not chilly, room to keep temperature down.
- Do not cuddle up to a feverish child despite your instincts to comfort; you will only make him hotter.
- Do give frequent sips of fluid to maintain hydration.
- Do take his temperature every 60–90 minutes and keep a record.

- Do sponge with *cool* water, starting with the forehead then the limbs and trunk to reduce temperature. Allow the water to evaporate on the skin, which will help to cool your child, or place him in a *lukewarm* shower or bath for a few minutes.
- Do not sponge him down with *cold* water because this causes blood vessels to contract, reducing heat loss.
- Do give paracetamol or ibuprofen in liquid form at the correct dosage at intervals as instructed on the box.
- Do contact your doctor if the temperature is persistent or fluctuating with troughs and high spikes.
- Do not let a child suffer a raised temperature for more than 24 hours without seeking medical advice.

When you call the doctor, describe the fever pattern from your records and any other symptoms. He will most likely ask you to come in, particularly if your child is very young.

FEBRILE CONVULSIONS

Febrile convulsions mostly affect children aged six months to six years, and occur in susceptible children in the early stages of a viral infection when the temperature is rapidly rising. Seizures can last between one and two minutes and can be particularly alarming for parents and carers. Follow Nanny's 'Fever Do's and Don'ts' (above) and always have your child checked by a doctor once he is over the seizure. If the seizure lasts for longer than one to two minutes, call for emergency help immediately. The obvious signs of a febrile convulsion are:

- Stiff body
- Loss of consciousness
- Twitching arms and legs

While a seizure is happening, place your child on his side so any vomit can dribble out, loosen clothing and sponge him with cool water from the head downwards. If you do need emergency help, do not leave your child alone. Pick him up and take him to the telephone with you.

NOTE ON EPILEPSY

This is hard to diagnose in small babies but it is a serious condition. Thankfully, it affects few children. However, any fit or seizure your child may suffer needs to be checked by a doctor to rule out the beginnings of epilepsy. Also consult your doctor if your toddler or pre-schooler has frequent losses of concentration that go beyond normal childhood day-dreaming.

TUMMY BUGS

Here is what to look out for if vomiting or diarrhoea set in.

Vomiting

This is going to happen at some point, whether it is because a child has eaten too much birthday cake or because he has picked up a tummy bug. If vomiting is illness-related, your child may have a raised temperature as well. All you can do is encourage rest and keep a bowl or bucket beside his bed or sofa. Lots of comfort, frequent sips of cooled boiled water and reassurance will help. If vomiting persists for more than 24 hours or has no obvious cause, you should seek medical advice. Projectile vomiting can happen when an older child loses control. Persistent projectile vomiting, projectile vomiting in tiny babies, or vomiting green bile in younger children should be treated immediately.

> ### NANNY'S TOP TIP
> Spraying shaving foam all over vomit on a carpet or fabric covering makes the vomit congeal, and it is then easily cleaned up with kitchen roll.

Diarrhoea

This can be a shock to your little one. A young child may need help in the toilet and reassurance. Offer lots of drinks to maintain hydration. Never give anti-diarrhoea drugs unless instructed to do so by a medical professional. A potty-training toddler might be persuaded to wear pull-up nappy pants for the duration of his tummy trouble to avoid accidents and upset, and if his diarrhoea continues at bedtime, a nappy and plastic sheet are essential.

Diarrhoea in babies is particularly distressing. In an especially bad bout, you can just be sticking down the tabs of a clean nappy when your baby goes again. Keep offering breast milk to maintain hydration, but if your baby is formula fed or already on cows' milk or similar, you may want to stop milk feeds and replace with cooled boiled water for a few hours to allow your baby's system to recover. Doctors recommend oral rehydration tablets, which offer a little sugar and salt. This aids absorption of water from drinks – but remember to check with your doctor first and follow the instructions on the box appropriate to the age of your child. Do not allow diarrhoea to continue in a baby under one year old for more than 24 hours, and eight hours is the limit for newborns as they are especially susceptible to dehydration.

Combined diarrhoea and vomiting in a tiny baby is serious and requires urgent medical help. He may be suffering from gastro-enteritis, in which case any home remedies are not going to cure the problem. Seek proper medical help quickly before your baby's condition becomes critical.

DEHYDRATION

This can come on rapidly in tiny babies. It is quickly recognised if:

- Your baby is lethargic
- Your baby has a dry mouth
- Your baby's fontanelle (top of his head) is sunken
- Your baby's eyes are sunken
- Your baby's skin feels loose
- Your baby is producing little urine

Seek urgent medical advice if your baby is very young; for older children offer frequent drinks and help your child to rest. To avoid dehydration on hot days, offer lots of drinks, even if your child does not think he needs them – thirst is a very delayed body reaction and he might be dehydrated and not realise.

CONSTIPATION

This can be a side-effect of illness. Equally, a small child too busy playing or unhappy going to the toilet alone at school can fail to listen to his body and become constipated. It can be a vicious circle of constipation leading to a sore bottom and therefore reluctance to try to go. The sooner you can help break this cycle the better.

Offer more drinks and provide extra fruit and vegetables at every meal to lubricate your child's digestive system. Try pure orange or apple juice for children; dilute with water for small babies over one year. Increased exercise can also help.

Constipation in a tiny baby is spotted by small pellets in his nappy or empty nappies. Your baby might draw up his knees to his chest if he is suffering tummy ache too. Gently massaging his tummy and helping him to exercise his legs can help.

If the problems persist ask your doctor or pharmacist for advice.

TUMMY ACHE

This can be alleviated by offering soothing drinks and perhaps a hot water bottle in a furry cover to cuddle. Tummy ache can happen because your child has rushed his supper or it may be associated with a current illness. However, acute tummy ache when your child is whimpering is not normal. Seek medical advice if you suspect anything serious.

HEADACHES

Headaches are rare in small children. They can be one of the early signs of dehydration, an illness or simply tiredness. It is best to offer more fluids and possibly pain relief at the correct dosage. Ask your child to sit quietly and calm down for a while. A headache could also be due to a drop in sugar levels so offer a glass of orange juice or half a banana. If a headache persists or worsens, seek medical advice.

COUGHS AND COLDS

Coughs with colds have different symptoms from coughs that might be croup or asthma. Here's what to look and listen for.

Colds

Although colds are pretty harmless and help to build up your child's immune system, you can take steps to avoid your family suffering too much. It is good practice to:

- put the hand over the mouth to protect others from coughs and sneezes
- wash hands after sneezing
- keep a large box of tissues to hand, and dispose of them after each use

Most colds disappear within five to seven days and do not need medication apart from a possible dose of liquid paracetamol to relieve a headache or low-grade temperature (follow the instructions on the box). All you can do to help your baby is offer him more drinks, allow time for rest and keep giving him a healthy diet full of vitamins.

Cold Sores

During winter, cracked lips and sore noses from constant blowing can become infected with a simple virus that causes 'cold sores'. You can spot the early signs around the nose or mouth when a raised red area appears. This may go on to form a blister and then a crusty scab. It is best to tackle cold sores while they are still at the red and tingly stage. You can buy antiviral creams over the counter at your pharmacist, but always let your pharmacist know what age child the cream is intended for.

Since cold sores are spread by contact, help your child to use only his own towel and wash his hands frequently, and try not to let him near other children – sharing kisses and runny noses will spread the virus. If a cold sore develops near your child's eye, then this is a matter for the doctor.

Croup

Croup has a distinctive sound: a hoarse cough, like a bark, and noisy breathing. It can be serious, so take your child to your doctor if:

- your child's skin is drawing in between his ribs at every breath
- he is irritable and restless
- he has blueness around his lips and face

These are serious symptoms and need immediate medical attention. However, normal croup can be alleviated by placing your child in a steamy room. The bathroom is best. Close the door and windows and run the hot tap to build up steam, and sit there together breathing in the warm moist air. It is difficult to play in a bathroom and books may get damp, so pass the time making up misty stories: 'Through the swirling mist I saw …'

ASTHMA

It is difficult for doctors to give a firm diagnosis of asthma in younger children because they cannot always perform the breathing tests required. However, many younger asthma sufferers grow out of it, or it might prove to be seasonal in response to an allergen. If your child has an asthma attack, try to pinpoint the trigger. It could be anything from pollens to new foods, infection or stress. Asthma symptoms are:

- persistent cough – worse at night-time or after exercise
- wheeze with the cough
- breathlessness – worse after running around

If your child has an attack, which is diagnosed by a doctor, you will be given correct medical advice specific to your child's condition. However, being asthmatic does not have to stop your child from dreaming of becoming an Olympic athlete. You, he and any other adults who care for him just need to know what can trigger an attack and how to cope with it.

Nanny's Asthma Management:
- Never panic – an asthmatic having an attack does not need the added stress.
- Carry any asthma medication at all times.
- Inform your child's friends, their parents and his nursery or school of his condition and what usually triggers it.
- Ask nursery or school to keep an inhaler in their medical chest clearly marked for your child's use.
- Talk to your child about what triggers his wheezes so that he can tell others what to help him avoid.

If your child understands how to behave during an asthma attack, then this can offer him the best help. All his carers should follow the same protocol.

Nanny's Asthma Attack Help:
- Sit your child on a straight-backed chair facing backwards, using the chair back to help him keep his chest and chin upright.
- Offer two puffs of reliever (or as prescribed to your child) through a spacer to have maximum effect.
- Allow five minutes and if breathing has not calmed, give another puff.
- Wait no longer than another 10 minutes before knowing when enough is enough and a doctor or emergency help is needed.

You should never exceed the prescribed dosage for your child's reliever because it can cause other problems. Your child should know how to use his inhaler and spacer combined, even if he cannot manage it himself during an attack. Practising at home on a teddy and then on himself will help in those times when your wheezing child has to rely on another adult to help him – he can show them how.

NANNY'S TOP TIP
Write the dosage in indelible marker pen on the outside casing of your child's inhaler – for example 'three puffs in three hours' – so that anyone helping him has immediate instructions and does not need to waste valuable time calling you.

Remember to clean inhalers regularly. They can get clogged up when the fine medication powder meets moisture in your breath. Dismantle the hard plastic covering from the inner medication cylinder and wash in warm soapy water. Allow it to dry naturally and pop the two units back together.

ALLERGIES

An allergy is an immune system response to an irritant. Allergies can take the form of skin rashes, hay fever with runny eyes and sneezes, or a tight chest and laboured breathing. Adults and children can develop allergies, but in children it can be quite distressing for them and you.

If you notice raised itchy weals on your child's skin (like severe nettle rash) and he is scratching them, think what he has come into contact with. Is it nettle rash or has he touched toxic plants or bulbs in the garden? Could he have sprayed your perfume on to his sensitive skin? Has he stroked a dog or cat and had a reaction to its fur? If you can identify the allergen all the better, so you can avoid it another time. In the meantime, if the reaction is mild, you should:

- Monitor your child, watching for any increase in the level of reaction.
- Keep your child cool, which will reduce itching, and dab with calamine lotion to soothe.

If the reaction continues, show your child's symptoms to a pharmacist who will prescribe the correct remedy or suggest you see a doctor if the condition is serious.

There is a short, easy-to-remember list of known allergens for small children:

- Nuts, particularly peanuts
- Seafood – shellfish, prawns, lobster, mussels

- Strawberries
- Honey

These allergens may not affect your child, but it is better to be safe than sorry, so it is not advised that your child eats nuts or shellfish until he is five when his body is more robust and able to cope if he does react. Strawberries and honey are less of a problem, but wait until your toddler is two before he indulges in these sweet treats.

You will not know your child is allergic until he suffers his first reaction, but you do need to know how to spot one. You are looking for:

- Constant itching
- Mild to serious rash
- Raised bumpy rash or weals
- Runny eyes and/or nose
- Persistent sneezes
- Tight chest and difficulty breathing

Anaphylactic Shock

This is the most serious form of allergic reaction and can progress from any of the above minor reactions if your child is susceptible. You can recognise this life-threatening condition if your child has:

- Swollen face
- Swollen tongue and mouth
- Difficulty swallowing
- Difficulty breathing
- Violent scratching at their neck

Anaphylaxis can be fatal, but an attack is reversible if treated quickly. So if you suspect anaphylactic shock, you *must* dial for emergency help immediately and *tell* the ambulance control room you think you are dealing with anaphylaxis. They will stay on the line with you to advise as the condition progresses, and you will get an absolute priority ambulance response.

Bee and Wasp Stings

Stings can cause an allergic reaction. Sometimes this can be mild with a localised swelling around the point of the sting, or it can become serious. Bee and wasp stings can be treated at home if mild.

Nanny's Sting Rules:

- Do not remove a bee sting by squeezing the venom sac. Instead, flick the sting out of the skin by placing your fingernail at the base of the sting where it enters the skin, avoiding the sac altogether.
- For bees and wasps, rub the immediate area vigorously once the sting has been removed. A good rub will release endorphins, your body's internal pain relievers, to the site of the sting.
- Apply an ice pack wrapped in a towel to reduce swelling.

Eczema

Allergic reactions can sometimes result in eczema. Changes in washing powder or reactions to woollen clothing are well-known triggers in susceptible children. Eczema is a skin condition that produces rashes and rough areas of skin that may crack and weep. It can be very itchy and sore, and usually affects the crooks of elbows, behind the knees and hands or face. There is nothing you can do to prevent eczema but you can help alleviate this scaly skin condition.

Nanny's Itch-reducing Advice:

- Use an emollient in your child's bath. Your doctor can prescribe something suitable.
- Use aqueous cream to wash him instead of soap.
- Reduce the number of baths to one or two per week since getting wet can exacerbate eczema.
- Give him cooler baths, not hot ones, to reduce the itchiness.
- Avoid bubble bath and detergents.
- Avoid man-made fabrics; cotton is best.

Always consult your doctor if this does not alleviate the symptoms. If your child's eczema is cracked and weeping, you will have to be extra vigilant for the possibility of infection in any open sores.

NANNY'S TOP TIP
Apply non-perfumed moisturiser to your child's skin in gentle downward strokes. Do not rub creams into eczema – this only promotes more itching.

Itching at bedtime can increase when your child gets hot under his bedclothes. This can disturb his sleep, so pop mittens on his hands and keep his fingernails as short as possible to avoid him ripping his skin. A pair of old long cotton socks with the feet cut off can be useful cylindrical bandages to slip over itchy knees or elbows.

Hay Fever
This seasonal allergic reaction causes a combination of sneezes, coughs, runny nose and watery eyes. It is caused by a reaction to anything from apple blossom to flower pollen to mown grass. It

is a miserable condition for sufferers so keep your child indoors during his personal hay fever season or give him an appropriate antihistamine remedy prescribed by your doctor.

NANNY'S TOP TIP

Buy your child a pair of fun sunglasses to wear during his hay fever season. They will help to prevent allergens irritating his eyes.

Infectious and Contagious Childhood Diseases

Many of the more serious diseases like measles, mumps and rubella are rare nowadays, but they still exist and may raise their ugly heads once again if parents fail to take advice on childhood inoculations. Here are the most common diseases Nanny has to deal with, and a checklist of the more serious diseases you need to recognise. They all require medical help.

CHICKENPOX

This raises its head generally between March and May and is spread by droplet infection from saliva and sneezes. It is a highly infectious disease, especially so two days before the rash appears. The incubation period is 11 to 21 days and the disease starts with feeling unwell, a rash and slight temperature. The rash develops into raised spots that look like blisters, which usually appear first on the chest and back then spread all over the body. They dry into scabs at which point the sufferer is no longer infectious; however, some childcare facilities will not take a child who still has spots, so expect about a fortnight out of nursery if your child attends one.

Do not pick the scabs off – your child might scar. Alleviate any temperature following Nanny's Fever Do's and Don'ts (see page 151), and if the scabs begin to itch, dab calamine lotion gently on to them with a non-fibrous clean cloth. Dress your child in loose pyjamas at night-time and pop cotton mittens on a smaller baby to prevent scratching in their sleep.

IMPETIGO

This spreads like raspberry jam at a children's tea party. It is transferred by direct contact and causes red skin with small blisters, which form a distinctive yellow or golden crust. It generally appears around the mouth and nose and is very uncomfortable around the eyes, and needs to be treated by your doctor. If your child is prescribed an ointment, then wear protective gloves when applying it. Keep your child away from nursery or school until his impetigo has cleared up, usually five days.

MENINGITIS

This relatively rare but very serious infection generally affects children under 16 years. In small children and babies, it can be particularly acute, which is why all parents and carers should recognise the early signals and know one simple test that will decide whether you are heading to hospital or just a routine trip to the doctor.

In *babies*, you are looking for:

- High-pitched moaning cry
- Difficult to wake or drowsy
- Refusing feeds
- Fever
- Loss of consciousness
- Red or purple spots which do not fade under pressure

In *older children*, you are looking for:
- Drowsiness, lethargy or confusion
- Severe headache
- Intolerance to bright light
- Stiff neck
- Fever
- Loss of appetite
- Red or purple spots which do not fade under pressure

You can investigate the rash by using a glass and carrying out the **Glass Test**: press the side of a glass against the rash. If the spots do not blanch or fade under pressure, call your doctor immediately, even if the other symptoms listed above are not all apparent.

Meningitis can progress swiftly, and symptoms that started out looking like a bad cold or flu can quickly become life threatening. It is important that you know the symptoms and carry out the glass test on *any* rash you notice on your child.

MEASLES
Measles takes seven to twelve days to incubate and starts with a bad cold and cough with sore eyes. Around day three to four a rash appears as the temperature rises.

MUMPS
This takes 7 to 12 days to incubate and starts with a fever and discomfort around the ears and throat. Swelling starts under the jaw with a temperature and general discomfort.

RUBELLA OR GERMAN MEASLES
This takes 14 to 21 days to incubate and starts with mild cold symptoms. A rash appears around day two.

Immunisations

Nowadays serious childhood diseases are fewer in number as immunisation programmes keep the worst offenders at bay. Your health visitor will explain the course of immunisations available to you and the reasons why your baby should have them. Your baby's immunisation programme will start at around three months and continue until he is in his mid-teens. The main injections given are:

- Diphtheria
- Tetanus
- Whooping cough
- Hib – a bacterial infection that can cause pneumonia, meningitis and blood poisoning
- Polio
- Measles, mumps and rubella – known as MMR
- Meningitis C
- Tuberculosis – known as BCG vaccination
- Hepatitis B

These are given at different ages and often with a booster, or renewed vaccination, at pre-school and teenage years. Taking your baby to his first vaccination session is never easy. You cannot prepare him for it, but you can give lots of love and cuddles afterwards. Rest assured, he will never remember the experience.

However, when your toddler goes for his injections, Nanny recommends truth and reward to help him through his appointment. Vaccinations do hurt; they do come as a shock to a child so expect his tearful eyes to look at you with real betrayal. Do your very best not to cry as well. Instead cuddle him, administer a treat like chocolate buttons and keep his favourite toy or comforter to hand. He needs some small reward for being a brave boy.

If you really think you cannot cope with holding your toddler still while he has his immunisations, then be honest and let the medical staff know. They would prefer to hold your child themselves and ensure the injection works first time than waste time and resources with both you and your child becoming increasingly flustered.

If your child has a fever on the day of his appointment, or has had previous bad reactions to vaccinations, then let your doctor know before you arrive. He may decide not to vaccinate until your child is better or he may be able to offer an alternative form of the same vaccine to avoid further bad reactions.

The whole point of immunisations is that they inject into our bodies a small dose of the illness to allow us to build up immunity. Sometimes, our bodies react by giving us a mild form of the illness so do keep an eye out for a raised temperature (anything over 38°C). Fevers over 39°C need to be seen by a doctor. Your pre-schooler's arm or thigh may be sore for a few days after his vaccinations; remember to let his nursery know he is tender so they can help him avoid rough play with his chums and can keep an eye on his temperature.

(For Nanny's advice on travel immunisations, see Chapter 2.)

Practical Guide to Childhood Accidents and Injuries

In this section, you will learn what to stock in your family's first aid kit, how to recognise injury in a young child and how to deal with breaks and bruises.

FAMILY FIRST AID KIT

If you did not possess one before your baby arrived, now is the time to head to the pharmacist and create your own first aid kit. You will also need to update an existing first aid kit to include items suitable for your baby.

Nanny's Home First Aid Kit:
- Age-appropriate painkillers and fever relief
- Medicine spoon and no-needle dosing syringe with stopper
- Thermometer
- Range of different-sized plasters
- Micro-pore sticky tape for holding down dressings
- Sterile gauze dressings for cuts and bad grazes
- Rolled and triangular bandages for sprains and support
- Antiseptic cream (check for allergies before using) or spray for cuts and grazes
- Calamine lotion for itchy rashes and sunburn
- Round-nosed scissors
- Tweezers for splinters and thorns, *not* stings
- Antiseptic wipes
- Small first aid manual to help if you forget

Remember to keep the first aid kit out of reach of your inquisitive child, but do let everyone in the family know where it is.

PLAYTIME INJURIES AND ACCIDENTS

As your child grows, he will be taking more risks, and with risk come inevitable tumbles, bumps and scrapes. It does not matter how many times Nanny has said 'don't run, don't jump', there are always tears in the early years. This is how to detect injuries in babies and smaller children.

Nanny's Breaks and Bruises Checklist:
- Is your child 'cuddling' his arm or not using it at all?
- Is your child not using a hand or finger when playing or eating?
- Is your child spending time hiding in corners or behind furniture?

- Is your child refusing to walk or crawl?
- Is your child whimpering when you pick him up?

If your child is hiding behind furniture, it may be because he knows no other way of dealing with this new painful experience. He may regress – for example, a learner walker will not limp but will revert to crawling or bottom-shuffling. This is a good indication that something might be wrong in one or both legs. Babies' bones are soft and pliable and do not readily break but accidents happen, so a child who winces on being picked up may have sore ribs or a broken collarbone. All signs of discomfort are worth checking out, but if you can readily link it to a certain knock or fall, seek medical assistance quickly.

If he cannot communicate verbally with you, ask your child to point to what is troubling him, but try not to ask leading questions. 'Where does it hurt?' is preferable to 'Is your knee painful?', even if you can see he is not happy walking or crawling. He might show you more than one 'hurt', and being too specific in your questions could mean you miss something. A shy child might be more comfortable showing you where teddy or dolly hurts than pointing to his own body. Older children should be able to answer your questions, but remember to be patient and let your child describe what is wrong at his own pace.

In her time, Nanny has witnessed the gamut of playtime injuries. As a parent, expect to deal with a range of the following – the more adventurous child should expect the lot!

Bites

Whether from an animal or, sadly, sometimes another child, bites need to be washed with clean, warm soapy water, and flushed out under constantly running water to ensure any debris in the wound is removed. Gently pat the wound dry and cover with a light gauze dressing until healed. If the bite is severe, grab any clean material to hand, form a pad from it and press firmly on to the bite while raising the wound above the heart if possible. This will help to slow the bleeding. Keep the wound covered and seek medical help.

Help your child avoid further injuries by telling him not to approach animals unless supervised by an adult, and emphasise to your child how much biting hurts and that he should not do it, even in retaliation.

Bruises

These are part of everyday childhood. Common areas for rainbow-coloured bruises are shins and bottoms: shins because children are too intent on their game to worry about painful knocks to this poorly designed part of the human body, and bottoms because children bump down stairs on their bottoms and fall off chairs when wriggling. However, serious bruises need attention. Press an ice pack covered in a towel on to the affected area and maintain pressure to minimise the swelling. If you notice bruises on your child that you or he cannot explain, it might be worth asking a few gentle questions about their cause.

Choking

This is a hazard for babies and children until they gain full control of their swallowing mechanism, and also learn not to bolt their food. If your baby is choking, making gasping noises and is unable to breathe, pick him up holding him along the length of your forearm with his face cradled into the palm of your hand. Tilt his head below the level of his body. Give five firm slaps to the middle of his back with the heel of your hand. This should dislodge whatever is causing the obstruction. Do not poke your fingers into his mouth to pull out anything you might be able to see; this could push the object further down. Instead, keep your baby face down and allow the object to drop out naturally.

If back slaps are not working, you will need to switch to abdominal thrusts. If your baby is under one year old, put him down on a firm surface, place your index and middle fingers on your baby's chest bone, approximately in the middle on a line between his nipples. Give five downward and forward careful thrusts, then check in his mouth for any obstruction. If this has not worked, repeat. Try another set of back slaps, and if you still have not succeeded, take your baby with you to the telephone and call an ambulance. Be prepared to give rescue breaths if your baby stops breathing.

Children over a year can be given back slaps by standing them up facing away from you. Support them around the waist with one arm whilst delivering five firm back slaps with the heel of your hand. Do not be scared of hurting your toddler because you need to do this firmly enough to stop the choking. Repeat the back slaps if your child has not coughed anything up. If you still cannot move the obstruction, move on to the Heimlich Manoeuvre. This is an abdominal thrust technique to be used only on children over one year old. Standing or kneeling behind your child, link your hands together under his arms, making a fist at the level of his belly button. Move your fist upwards until it is half way between his button and his breastbone. Now pull inwards and upwards quickly, and check your child's mouth after each thrust. Do not let choking continue beyond a minute before you call for emergency help.

Cuts, Scrapes and Grazes

If your child plays rough, climbs trees or jumps walls, a scabby knee is his likely reward. Once your child has calmed down, head to the first aid box. Follow the procedure for bites, as above. Remember to check for any gravel or dirt in the cut, and flush out with running water. Never use cotton wool to clean a graze because the wound will have a rough surface that will attract bits of fluff. Seek medical help if the wound is severe. Now administer a medicinal glass of juice and a biscuit, and let your child get straight back to climbing trees.

NANNY'S TOP TIP

Never let children run with a sweetie lolly in their mouth. If they fall over while sucking it, they may choke.

Head Injuries

These need to be treated with great care. The first thing to do is sit your child down, ask him how it happened and apply a cold compress to the bump. Check his head for any sign of a cut and treat this accordingly. If he appears at all confused, monitor him for five minutes, and if his condition does not change, then call a doctor for advice. If your child was unconscious when you found him or you are told by his friend that he knocked himself out, then he must be seen by a doctor immediately. The doctor will give you advice on concussion and how to monitor your child's progress.

Nosebleeds

Get your child to lean forwards, letting the blood drip down away from clothes and preferably into a bowl or basin on the floor. Do not let him lean backwards because blood can flow down the throat and cause choking or vomiting. Pinch your child's nostrils between thumb and forefinger and ask him to breathe through his mouth. Pinch for about 10 minutes to allow clots to form. Soothe your child to keep him calm, but wait until the bleeding has stopped before you ask him to answer your main question: 'How did it happen?' You may need to think about a possible break. If the bleeding has not stopped after 20 minutes and continues to flow freely, take lots of old tea towels with you to keep mopping up and get to a doctor.

Nanny strongly advises that your child refrains from nose picking for a few days to give the scabs inside his nostrils a chance to heal.

Splinters

Tackle splinters using a pair of sterilised tweezers. You can sterilise them by holding them in the flame of a match or dipping for a few seconds in boiling water. Clean the wound with a wet wipe or soap and water, explain to your child clearly what is going to happen, then place the tweezers as close to the skin as possible and pull the splinter out at the same angle as it went in. Squeeze your child's finger to ooze out a few drops of blood to make sure that any dirt under the skin is forced out. Then cover with a plaster. Remember, some children are allergic to plasters so do check before applying one.

Sprains

Sprains are injuries to the softer tissues, muscles and tendons. They are relatively rare in flexible younger children, but if you suspect a sprain – recognisable by pain, swelling and bruising of a joint – then the simple rule to follow is: RICE

Rest
Ice
Compression
Elevation

and, if necessary, a firm bandage to support the joint until it heals.

SERIOUS ACCIDENTS WILL HAPPEN ...

Nanny hopes serious accidents never happen. However, you need to know what to do when rough and tumble play goes too far, or adults take their eye off the ball and child.

Broken Bones

These come in two forms – greenstick fractures and compound fractures. Under X-ray, a greenstick fracture looks just like a green twig that has snapped. It is partly bent and splintered on the convex side of the bend. In a compound fracture, the bone fractures completely and is in two pieces. Because his bones are still flexible, your child is more likely to have a greenstick fracture. Whichever form of break he has suffered, you need to keep your child calm and prevent him from moving the affected part of his body. He may be in shock and will need a lot of comfort while you get him to the hospital. Do not give him anything to eat or drink because he may need an anaesthetic when the surgeons set his bones.

In the worst case, if the broken bone is poking through the skin, then cover the open wound with a clean and non-fibrous cloth such as muslin, and apply pressure *around* the wound to slow the bleeding. Do not press on the bone itself. It is probably best to lie your child down since he is likely to start showing signs of shock. It is almost impossible to drive a child who is bleeding and in pain to an emergency department on your own, so if a neighbour or partner cannot help, call an ambulance and concentrate on comforting your child until medical help arrives.

Ribs can snap during excessive boisterous play. Your child may show signs of pain when you pick him up or have a cuddle, and he may find it painful on every breath. If he is slowing down, reluctant to play and avoids cuddles, take him to your doctor for a check-up.

Burns and Scalds

Treat minor burns by removing any clothing covering the burn and holding the affected limb under cold running water for 10 minutes to take the heat out of the skin. Cover the wound with a sterile gauze dressing or a non-fibrous pad and bandage loosely to allow air to help the burn to heal. Blisters might form, but do not be tempted to pop them. They are the body's own form of burn treatment. If one bursts by accident, cover it with a clean dressing.

More serious scalds or burns need medical help. Call an ambulance first, then hold the affected body part under cold running water. Do not remove any clothing that may be stuck to a serious burn. After 20 minutes of cold water, wrap the wound in a single layer of cling film. This will keep any dust or dirt out, helping to avoid infection. Cover a facial burn with a clean non-fibrous cloth. While you wait for medical help, give lots of comfort. Remember, butter or grease of any form should *not* be rubbed into any burn or scald. It will only fry the affected skin.

Drowning

Drowning means inhaling water after being submerged, whether it be in the bath, a pond, a pool or open water. If it is safe to do so, rescue your child and carry him to dry land with his head downwards to avoid further inhalation of water or vomit in his lungs. If he is unconscious and not breathing, give resuscitation as described on pages 139 and 140 (Practical Guide to Medical Emergencies) and call an ambulance.

Electric Shock

This happens rarely, particularly if all electrical sockets are covered. However, if it does occur you should first ensure it is safe for you to approach. Switch off the power at the mains, or use a wooden broom or chair (anything that does not conduct electricity) to separate your child from the electricity supply. Stand on a book to protect yourself from the current. Once the connection has been broken, check your child to see if he is breathing and look for any burns. Always give resuscitation first and then treat burns with cold water and cover with clean non-fluffy material while you wait for an ambulance.

Hypothermia

Although it sounds like it could never happen in the home, babies and children cannot control their body temperature like adults, and cold can set in unnoticed. Even if your baby has nicely pink cheeks, if his skin is cold to the touch and he is floppy and quiet and not feeding, then he may be too cold and on the margins of hypothermia. You must call your doctor. While you are waiting for him to arrive, move to the warmest room in your home, pop a hat on your baby and cuddle him wrapped in a blanket. Gradual warming through body contact is the best kind of warmth you can offer.

Toddlers and older children can tell you when they are getting cold, but if they are engrossed in playing, they may not realise they are shivering violently. Swimming for too long or playing outside on a windy day are the more common causes of hypothermia in small children. They simply forget they need to come indoors or ask for another jumper. An extra layer and a hot drink will help warm him up. However, full hypothermia can come on quickly. If you notice your child's skin becoming pale, the edge of his mouth turning blue and if he is shivering and slightly confused, then you must seek medical help. While you wait, put more clothes on him including a hat and get into bed together under the duvet.

Poisoning

The most common cause of poisoning in children is swallowing something toxic that has not been put away properly. The best method of prevention is to keep anything poisonous out of reach.

If the worst happens and your child has swallowed household chemicals or taken a handful of tablets, and is showing signs of confusion, vomiting and altered breathing, then call for emergency help. Do not give anything to eat and drink, and try to locate the source of the poison because the hospital will need to know:

- What has been taken
- When it was taken
- How much has been taken

Try to give medical staff your child's accurate weight. This will help them decide which treatment to offer.

Common Infestations

You would like to think it is you and your child who go visiting, but sometimes your little one may have visitors all of his own. Your child has a waterproof outer coating – his skin – but every now and then his defences can come under attack from worms, skin diseases and crawlies. Keeping your child clean, particularly in his creases and folds, will help, but once he starts nursery or school, the likelihood of little visitors increases. Most childcare facilities have a policy asking those with infestations to remain at home until they are clear, but sadly it is often too late and your child and his chums have already shared their tiny friends. Here are Nanny's worst wriggling and lousy enemies and how to send them packing.

HEAD LICE
Head lice are not fussy; they will live in any child's hair. They move from head to head by crawling between toddlers intent on sharing a game with their heads touching. Nits are the eggs the lice lay in the hair – tiny white-grey lozenges stuck to the roots, generally behind the ears and round the temples. If your child is

incessantly scratching these areas or you notice tiny pepper dots, the lice's droppings, on his pillow, then you need to check your child's head carefully.

Once you have a confirmed case – and most schools will have spotted them already and sent home a note to parents – you need to treat your child's hair. Nanny avoids chemical remedies and prefers to use a comb:

- Wash his hair and leave in lots of conditioner.
- Take a fine-toothed comb and, working from the roots, slowly comb out the lice and nits (the conditioner makes the hair slippery and the lice come unstuck).
- Clean the comb between every stroke by wiping it on a piece of tissue.
- Continue combing, sectioning his hair until you have covered everywhere.
- Wash his hair again.
- Repeat every two to three days for a fortnight.

Intense itching is caused by the lice biting, so check for signs of infection in your child's scalp and comb regularly, remembering to check your own head and anyone else in the family too. Long-term infestation can cause lack of sleep, low energy and generally make your child feel lousy!

NANNY'S TOP TIP

In the old days, Nanny used to treat the entire nursery in one go. If you can persuade all the parents in your child's class and get signed permission slips, have a whole class nit session. A couple of parents can treat everyone's heads in one hit after school one afternoon.

WORMS

These come in various forms – the main varieties you may encounter are threadworms, ringworms and roundworms. They are thankfully not life threatening, but they are not nice and need to be dealt with at the first sign of infestation.

Threadworms

These live in your child's intestines. You might see their tiny white threads in your child's poo, or he might have a persistent itch around his bottom that is particularly bad at bedtime. To get rid of an infestation, ask your doctor to treat the entire family because you are all likely to be housing lodgers. Threadworms get around by laying eggs, which find their way under your child's nails; he then sucks his fingers and the cycle of worm to egg starts again. So to help your child evict his visitors, Nanny recommends:

Nanny's Worm Rules:

- Keep fingernails very short.
- Wash hands frequently and definitely before eating.
- Take nightly baths to maintain a clean bottom.
- Ensure your child wears pyjamas at night to help prevent him having direct contact when scratching the uncontrollable itching around his bottom.
- Disinfect the toilet seat after every visit until the infestation is eradicated.
- Vacuum bedrooms and wash bed linens on a hot cycle.
- Treat the whole family.

Roundworm or Toxocara

Roundworm comes from dogs and foxes, and is found in their faeces. This is why children's play areas in parks are fenced off. Roundworm can affect your child's brain, eyes, lungs, kidneys and muscles if left untreated. Symptoms are a cough, pale skin, tiredness, not thriving and an urge to eat weird foods like coal or soil. Dogs become immune to roundworm at six months; if you have a new puppy, you need to worm him because toddlers and puppies share a lot of germs by licking things and playing on the carpet. Follow Nanny's basic worm hygiene rules (see above), and add these few extra to cope with roundworm:

- No licking
- No puppies in your child's sandpit
- No dog fouling in public places

Ringworm

This is actually a fungal infection commonly found on children's faces and scalps. On the head, it appears flaky; on the face it forms reddish ovals or rings with inflamed edges, and it is quite itchy. Animals get it too, which can be the source of your toddler's infection. So, Nanny's 'Worm Rules' still apply (see above) and add the following to prevent the spread of ringworm:

- No swapping hats
- No sharing hairbrushes
- No trying on each other's clothes

Ask the vet to treat your dog.

Warts and All

WARTS

Warts are small hard growths on the skin caught by contact with an infected person. They can be unsightly and painful, in which case ask your pharmacist's advice for treatment.

> **NANNY'S TOP TIP**
> Dab apple cider vinegar on warts three times a day. The wart disappears in under two weeks. This is much better than using chemicals on young children.

VERRUCAS

These are warts on the feet, usually picked up in sports changing rooms. They appear on the sole of the foot as little black specks, but can become painful as they expand and your child walks on them. You can get over-the-counter verruca remedies, and your child should wear plastic socks in barefoot situations until his infection clears up.

ATHLETE'S FOOT

This fungal infection loves sweaty toes and can affect the most sedentary child. Symptoms are itchy, cracked skin, which can become sore and flaky. Treat with athlete's foot powder applied after a bath when feet have been thoroughly dried and left to air. Wear cotton socks, leather or canvas shoes, or sandals if your child has particularly sweaty feet. Lots of fresh air should clear it up in one or two weeks. Once your child has had it, it is best to keep an eye on his feet for further infection to catch it early.

Sun Safety

Nanny cannot think of a better reminder to stay safe in the sun than:

- **Slip** on a T-shirt
- **Slap** on a hat
- **Slop** on sunscreen

The worst part of the day for sun damage is between 11am and 3pm. During this time, keep your baby totally out of the sun, and help toddlers and older children to cover up and head for the shade.

The shoulders, face, back of neck and tops of ears are the most obvious areas for sunburn so slop on lots of high-factor sunscreen and stay in the shade until the sun is less fierce later in the afternoon.

Nanny recommends children wear a sun hat at all times on sunny days. Baby sun hats should have a tie under the chin to help it stay on; children's sun hats get Nanny's tick of approval if they have a sewn-in neck flap like a legionnaire's hat. Sunglasses for children on holiday are a good idea to protect their eyes from the glare, especially near water where the damage from the sun's reflecting rays can go unnoticed. Use waterproof sunscreen if your child is going swimming. You can also buy lightweight wet suits or rash vests that are sun proof and cover your child's body from neck to knees.

A morning application of sunscreen does not last all day, so remember to apply more when you venture back outside after your middle of the day shade break.

SUNBURN

Sunburn is painful and unnecessary. If your child is unfortunate enough to suffer sunburn, take him indoors, keep him cool and dab his sore skin with calamine lotion from a non-fibrous pad. Do not use cotton wool as it may stick to his burnt skin. He will need lots of drinks to rehydrate and he might need pain relief to ease the discomfort. Once burnt, you should keep your child totally out of the sun until his skin has healed.

HEATSTROKE

This is a serious condition caused by prolonged exposure to the sun. Your child may show signs of fever, loss of appetite and drowsiness and generally feel very unwell. You can help by giving him lots of fluids and calling a doctor.

Nanny hopes your family will never experience half of what she knows about childhood illnesses and injuries. However, now you are armed with Nanny's common-sense approach to all things medical, your little one can grow up happy, healthy and bursting with life, fully equipped to do what children do best – play.

CHAPTER 6
playtime with nanny

Play is important to your child's physical, sensory and intellectual development. It is through play that your child makes sense of the world around him, and play encourages imagination, cooperation, sharing and creativity – all skills he will need when he grows up. As adults, we often forget how to play, and even the most fun-loving parent needs some practical suggestions for games and activities, so this chapter sets out to inspire you and your child at playtime, both indoors and outdoors. It will give you hints on how to set up a playroom and avoid the television, and suggest some imaginative and fun ways to wile away a few hours with cheap and easy games and pastimes.

Play Space and Play Things

Try to create a space at home where your child can play. It might be a spare room, which can be transformed into a playroom, or it might be his bedroom. It needs to be somewhere where he can leave games and toys out – somewhere he feels is his own special place. If space is limited, think about setting aside a corner of one room as his play area where he can keep his toys.

Many parents go over the top with toys, but Nanny's approach is not to have too many and keep them simple. If chosen carefully, toys can encourage leaps in development. They can help him develop his fine motor skills and solve problems; they can encourage spatial awareness and get him thinking about colours, shapes, numbers and letters, so choose them wisely.

We live in a technology-obsessed age but very young children haven't changed that much. They still like building bricks, puzzles, train sets and colouring books, and the under fives won't want computer games or MP3 players unless you encourage them. Wooden toys are a good buy as they last longer and can be passed on to siblings or relatives when they are no longer needed. Children do not need the latest toy on the market, and most psychologists agree that buying expensive, flashy toys is often about parents wanting to get their children what everyone else has, so don't bow to pressure. That expensive toy quad bike may make daddy feel like a racing driver, but it will do nothing for your child, apart from make him expect large and expensive toys.

Pick toys that are appropriate for the age of your child. There must be no rough edges, no flaking or toxic paint and no strings to ensnare little fingers or to strangle. Nanny recommends you always wash or wipe down toys every week, especially if any of the children, or their friends, have coughs or colds. Warm soapy water is fine. Whatever you decide to buy, the one thing you must ensure is that the toy is safe.

Nanny's Toy Safety Checklist:
- Always make sure toys carry a safety standard mark.
- Always check the age range for the toy. By law, toy manufacturers have to mark their toys if they are not suitable for children under three years.
- Check that all toys have no sharp edges or small parts that may be a choking hazard.

PLAY MATES

Learning how to make friends is one of the most important aspects of play. When your child is a baby, he will play alone and take little notice of other children. It is not until children are around four years old that they start playing together. Despite this, it is good for your child to get used to playing with, or alongside, other children from an early age, even if he ignores them. If the local 'mother and toddler' group isn't your cup of tea, try and take your child along to a baby music class, swimming, to friends with similar aged children or try a playgroup session. This may be his first opportunity to socialise with people who aren't his family, and getting him used to mixing with other children now will help him adapt to nursery and school when he is older.

Play Time

Nanny always structures play so that morning is the time for thinking and learning activities when a child's ability to concentrate is greater. High-energy activities and games are scheduled for the afternoon when the child needs to let off steam and his attention span is shorter.

Letting your child have 'down time' to play at home is very important. Some parents fill their children's time with outings, events and classes, giving them no time to play on their own. Quiet playtime or 'free play' is key to a child's emotional development. This doesn't mean sitting them in front of the television or computer; it means time for unstructured play – time to paint, make Lego or play on their own with their toys. A big problem with providing constant activity and events for your child is that he will get to the point where he finds it increasingly difficult to amuse himself. So overdoing the extracurricular activities means you are creating a rod for your own back – and you are far more likely to hear the dreaded exclamation – 'MUMMY I'M BORED!' So build in time each day where your child has free play.

You can encourage free play by not interfering too much in your child's games; this will help him concentrate and develop his imagination in his own way. Norland College supports the approach of Maria Montessori, a trained doctor and the founder of the Montessori schools. At Montessori schools, children are allowed to work as long as they like on a game or play activity, and adults do not interrupt or shunt them from one activity to another. This approach has been shown to promote greater levels of concentration. Try not to interrupt your child; if you want to join in with his play, show interest in what your child has been doing, rather than diverting him. You can do this by asking questions about his game: 'How much tea is teddy drinking? Where is your train travelling to?' Remember to discuss his game with him after he has finished. Children love to be with adults who understand play at their level.

TV OR NOT TV?

Quiet time for many parents means sitting the children in front of the box. How much time a child should spend watching television or playing computer games is always an interesting discussion point among carers and parents. Research has shown that too much television is a bad thing for a child's development and Nanny couldn't agree more. Many parents use the television as a 'babysitter', sitting their child in front of it to keep them quiet but this will create problems for you and your child as they get older. Your little one will get so used to sitting passively in front of the screen that he will lose the habit of playing on his own, using his imagination, exercising or making friends. Modern society is dominated by the visual media but Nanny knows that when a child is very young, no television is best. The American Academy of Paediatrics has demonstrated that the more television young children watch, the more likely they are to have trouble paying attention and concentrating during their early school years.

However, Nanny is going to be realistic here. If you do choose to use the television to gain some quiet time, then use DVDs because you have control over the content and duration of the programme.

SUGAR AND SPICE, AND ALL THINGS NICE ...

Whether we like it or not, there is a difference between the way boys and girls play. However, this is no excuse for stereotyping, so always cook with your sons and show your daughters how to use a spanner. As a parent, you should make sure that you show your child that there are gender differences, but that gender roles are very flexible; that way none of his play becomes stereotypical. You can help your child when he is younger by allowing him freedom to play with any toy; this is easier if you have children of different gender. Let him play freely with both girls' and boys' toys. Learning the differences between the sexes is a natural part of growing up.

TEACHING MUMMY AND DADDY TO PLAY

As parents or carers, we are often busy with family and work commitments. It's a rush to get through the day and get everything done. However, make sure you set aside some time to play with your child every day. Most child experts will tell you that simply spending some quality time having fun together, playing a game or reading a book, is one of the best things that you can do. It lets your child know that you value him and that you enjoy spending time with him. With every bounce on a trampoline, every cup of tea drunk at a teddy bears' picnic and every hour spent making cardboard robots, you are helping to raise a happy, well-adjusted child.

You would be surprised how many parents don't know how to play with their children. This is probably why some parents end up compensating by buying too many toys. So remember, sometimes your child simply wants to play with *you*. Your child loves routine, so if he knows that he gets to read a book with mummy in the morning before work and that Saturday morning is daddy's playtime, that trains you as parents to build in family time as well. Don't be distracted – let the mobile ring, reschedule any of your commitments to after bedtime – now is your child's special time with mummy and daddy.

So what sort of games can you play, and how do you make a stimulating home environment where the children can amuse themselves without slumping in front of the television or computer? Here are some ideas to make playtime fun. For ease of reference, Nanny has split the rest of the chapter into two sections: 'The Great Indoors' and 'The Great Outdoors'.

The Great Indoors

THE DRESSING-UP BOX

Nanny's favourite item for the playroom is the dressing-up box. It provides endless hours of creativity and games. Be imaginative when putting it together; any item of old clothing or footwear can be adapted, and accessories are good too. So, a black wrap or shawl makes a great vampire cape; grandpa's old hat and jacket can become a clown's outfit, and cheap sparkly jewellery and beads make great pirate treasure or princess trinkets. Become a magpie and your box will be an instant hit with the under fives.

Nanny's Dressing-up Box Essentials:
- Junk jewellery
- Handbags
- Bracelets
- Old hats
- A few pieces like pirate hats, witches' hats and fairy wings bought from a toyshop
- Old clothes
- Sunglasses
- Old material – especially patterned, fake fur or shiny
- Old shoes – especially mum's party shoes

Remember, don't throw anything away. Even though you think your child may have grown out of the dressing-up stage, you can guarantee there will be times when the dressing-up box comes in useful, such as for fancy dress parties, Halloween or school productions. If you have kept all the jumble, you will be able to pull a fairy or pirate costume out of the box.

Shiver Me Timbers! How to Make a Pirate Costume

Nanny always prefers to make costumes rather than buy them. It helps if you have a flair for sewing but it's not essential, so start planning early and include your child in the creative process. Making a new costume can be a fun way for you and your little one to spend a wet afternoon together. Here's a quick and easy way to transform your child into a budding Blackbeard the Pirate.

Cut a pair of old trousers (black or red) raggedly below the knee, add a stripy T-shirt or draw a skull and crossbones on a plain one. With an older child, you can search for designs online or in books, which allows you to discuss your costume, its history and its design. Your child might want to draw a pirate pattern, flag or design for himself. Make a cutlass shape from cardboard and cover in silver paper. An eye patch can be made out of a piece of black card or felt and some elastic, and add a spotty or red scarf as a bandana. Your little buccaneer is ready to splice the mainbrace and head off to Treasure Island …

LET'S PRETEND …

'Let's pretend' is not just about dressing up and playing at being a princess or pirate; younger children love to re-enact real events they have experienced too. Playing at shops or going to the post office can keep a small child occupied for hours. Role-play has unlimited potential and you can tailor it to your child's interests. You could set up a train station (especially if you have a toy train set), a tea shop/café, a shoe shop, the vets (all those sick cuddly toys!) or a hairdressers (brushing and styling only). These games are guaranteed to keep your child – and you – occupied for hours. Here are some ideas for simple everyday role-play games:

The Corner Shop
Set up a shop using old cardboard boxes, cereal packets and cartons. You and your child play at being a shopkeeper and customer. Use a basket or bag for your 'produce'. You can even use price tags to get your child to think about numbers and money. Use play money or pennies, and ask your child to count out how many pennies are needed for payment or for change.

The Builders
You will need a pen and paper for house design, hard hats, tape measure, toy telephone or old mobile phone and building blocks. Discuss your 'new' house with your child, then measure up the site, draw up your designs and build it out of play bricks. There will be lots of phone calls about numbers of bricks needed and the colour of the front door. Remember, the more you throw yourself into the role, the more fun it will be.

TELL ME A STORY
Every parent knows how important reading is to a child. From a very early age most children love stories and books. Nanny recommends you start reading to your child from day one. If he grows up constantly hearing stories, whether he can understand them or not, he will learn to love books. Just let the words he doesn't know wash over him like music. Reading books to your child, no matter how young he is, becomes part of his routine and he becomes used to hearing a huge range of words. It also helps develop his language skills and promotes a wide vocabulary. If your child can express himself well, he is less likely to become frustrated, and so

if you interact and ask questions when reading, your child will develop the ability to talk about what he hears.

As your child grows, ask him to join in with sounds as you read – he could moo when there is a cow or bark when there is a dog – or get him to answer questions about the stories: why did Jack and Jill go up the hill? How did Humpty feel when he fell off the wall? Or describe the scene to him and ask him about the pictures: look at the penguins – do you think their feet get cold living in the snow?

NANNY'S TOP TIP

Let toddlers turn the pages themselves – it often makes them more interested in the books if they feel they have control. Help them to know when, by using your finger to point to the words as you reach the last sentence.

Not all parents are great storytellers, but you can enhance your performance by making the story as dramatic as possible using accents, funny voices and props – and remember your child thinks you are fantastic, so don't worry about bad acting. At school, your child will have to read aloud as part of the curriculum and so expression in reading is an important part of his education. That's why you need to show him how to do it by making sure each character has an individual voice and your reading is full of life. Listen to some audio books, which you can download from the web, to give you some inspiration.

Another way of bringing the story to life is by using toys. Tell the story as a puppet show with your child or as a theatre play with older children. You can paint scenery on paper and, if you have space, even hang up a sheet on some string as the curtain. You could make a 'story box' where you store props and hand puppets that you know go with certain favourite stories. Be creative with the story; ask your child to help tell it. Create alternative endings or discuss what he would do if faced by a wolf in a forest or a prince who was a frog, or if he found a beanstalk in the garden. Add your own little flourishes and make it part of the story to see if he can spot the deviations in his favourite tales.

NANNY'S TOP TIP

Use photography, art, history or wildlife books – anything with interesting pictures – to encourage your child to look at the wider world beyond fairytale images in children's books.

If you haven't got a range of picture books, visit the local library. Many libraries run children's story time sessions so make sure you know what's on. If you introduce your children to the library early, they will easily be able to spend an hour or two looking at books when they are older, and it often buys you a little quiet time too. A way to make a trip to the library fun is to set yourself a project – dinosaurs, the weather, sea creatures, anything that your child is interested in – and make a scrapbook or journal.

FIND THE ALPHABET

Once your child has developed a love of words and is starting to learn the alphabet, you can try the ABC game. This can be adapted for indoors or outdoors. You and your child have to go round the house or garden and find an object that begins with the letter of the alphabet, starting with A then B then C and so on. Small objects are best as you can lay them out on the floor or table. Make it fun by adding some treats such as S is for sweetie or B is for biscuit and they get to eat that 'letter' once you have finished your alphabet. It might be worth some forward planning for X and Z so you could have a xylophone or a toy zebra, but if not, find a picture of one in a book or on the computer.

This is also a great game for art galleries and museums. Ask your child to find an animal beginning with L ... you know it's a lion and he finds it, then an object that begins with M ... and so on. Another idea is to make a list of 10 things you have to find in the gallery (such as a train, a tree, a boat) and then look for them in the paintings or objects. This is a wonderful introduction to art and museums, and encourages your child to observe and discover.

MAKE A TREASURE BASKET

One of Nanny's favourite play items for younger children is the treasure basket. This is a wonderful low-cost 'toy basket' for children of all ages, but particularly for babies who can sit confidently on their own. None of the objects placed in the basket are 'purchased' toys; the aim is to attract your child's interest through touch (texture, shape, weight), smell, sound and sight (colour, length, shininess). A treasure basket encourages a baby to discover things for himself. Here's what you need:

Nanny's 'Little Treasure's' Treasure Basket
You will need a flat-bottomed, shallow-sided basket; the best height is about 12 centimetres. It needs to be the right size, as your child must be able to sit beside it and reach inside. Fill the basket with objects that have a range of textures, colours and shapes for baby to investigate. For a 12-month-old baby, the basket could contain the following:

- Rough and smooth fabrics – felt and hessian are good textures
- A piece of natural sponge or loofah
- Fir cones without seeds

- Nail brush
- Larger sea shells (large enough not to be swallowed)
- Tin foil already scrunched up
- Wooden spoon and mug or beaker
- Lavender bag
- Plastic container with buttons inside (for rattling)
- Laminated pictures of eyes, ears, noses, mouths or members of the family
- Cotton reels or corks threaded on short strings
- Clothes pegs
- Mirror (plastic for safety)
- Ball of wool

Your treasure basket can hold anything you can find around the house (not toys) that might be fun for your child to touch and feel, but make sure you select objects with safety in mind. Do not include small or sharp objects, and plastic should be avoided. Keep an eye on your child while he explores. Introduce new objects and your baby will be delighted by fresh discoveries in his treasure basket. The basket is about exploration, concentration and the first steps in decision-making.

NANNY'S TOP TIP

Place your child sideways on to the basket, so that he can reach in and take items out and then place them on the floor on his opposite side. If he sits facing the basket directly, he won't be able to reach everything inside it and may even topple forwards into it.

If you have two children sitting at the treasure basket, encourage them to share objects. Cooperative play comes naturally when children are about four years old, but you can show them how to share when they are babies.

NANNY'S TOP TIP

Encourage sharing during a play date by playing pass and thank you games. Ask your baby to share an object from the basket, passing it to his friend and back again.

As your baby grows you can create other games using the treasure basket. Here are some ideas for using some of the objects as sensory games:

Mirror Mirror on the Wall

What you need: A mirror (plastic not glass, for safety).
What you do: Sit on the floor with your baby and make sure you are both reflected in the mirror.

This is a good game for young babies. Ask questions and answer for him by actions, gestures and words. For example, you ask 'Where's your mouth?' You answer 'There's your mouth!' and point to it on the mirror and on your face. Similarly, you could say 'Where's mummy's nose? There's mummy's nose!' You can extend this to include expressions: 'Is mummy happy?' (smile). 'Yes! Mummy and baby are happy.' 'Are mummy and baby silly?' (pull a face). 'Yes! Mummy and baby are silly!' Young babies love this game and it helps develop their vocabulary and self-awareness. Be prepared to play it for some time! It's a great one for long train journeys or sitting waiting in surgeries, as it just requires a mirror in your handbag.

What's in the Bag?

What you need: A pillowcase and some toys and objects from the treasure basket such as fir cones and cotton reels

What you do: Place 10 objects in the pillowcase. The objects need to be familiar items to your child such as a cuddly toy, a building brick, a ball, a fir cone, a straw. Ask your child to feel inside the bag and guess what the objects are. Can he guess what's in the bag? What does it feel like? Soft? Hard? This game helps to encourage his sense of touch and his memory.

TAKE ART

Creativity is one of the things that makes us human. No other mammal can make things that express ideas or feelings. This desire to create begins very early. Children love creative play, be it making a collage or creating a stick house. Give your child cardboard, paint, stickers, paper or crayons and you will stimulate his imagination. You will also help him to develop fine motor skills as he learns to hold brushes, pencils and other tools.

Nanny is always prepared for artistic endeavours and has a 'rainy day box' full of craft items. Inside is everything needed to make collages, puppets and pictures and encourage creative play. It

> These are the contents of my rainy day box: ribbon, string, wool, plain paper, coloured paper, numbers and letters written on card, envelopes, postcards, foam shapes, dice, colouring book, colouring pencils, glue stick, playing cards, shoelaces, small basket, stickers, pegs, pipe cleaners, material, bows, labels. I keep all my items in a bright blue box bought from a local stationer's, but you could decorate an old box yourself. It continues to grow as new things are added and improved.
> **Nanny Emily**

also includes items that will help children learn how to tie shoelaces or count coins. This is an incredibly useful box, as you instantly know where all your art and craft items are – the glue, the paint, the sticky tape – and you can get straight down to making things.

Here are some of Nanny's ideas for things to make from your rainy day box.

Envelope Puppets

What you need: Envelopes (big enough to fit over your hand – an A5 brown or white envelope is best), glue stick, buttons, gold braid, silver foil, sequins, paper clips, pipe cleaners, wool.

What you do: Use the envelope as the basis for the puppet – you will be placing this over your hand when it is finished. You and your child can make any character you like by sticking on cotton wool for hair, buttons for eyes, thin card or felt for mouths and clothes. You could use silver paper to make a puppet robot, or use felt tips or paints to draw puppet animals.

Monster Sock Puppets

Perfect for all those odd socks we all seem to end up with. If you are practical, you can sew the accessories on to the sock, but otherwise you can use glue.

What you need: A long sock, glue, felt, cardboard, buttons, wool and anything else useful from your rainy day box.

What you do: The completed puppet will be placed over your hand with the heel of the sock on your knuckles. It's worth putting the sock on your hand before you start sewing to work out where you need to put everything. Sew two buttons just below the heel for eyes. Cut 10-cm lengths of wool for hair and stick or sew them above the eyes. Cut out a red tongue and sew it to the toe of the sock. You could also cut white felt teeth and sew these around the tongue. When you place it on your hand, push the toe area into the palm of your hand to make a mouth.

Straw Necklace

What you need: Several large-diameter paper drinking straws and a piece of string.

What you do: Cut the drinking straws into 3-cm sections. Place on a tray. Tie a knot in the end of the string and ask your child to thread the straw pieces on to the string. A variation of this is to paint the straws in red, blue and yellow and then get your child to thread the straws in a pattern. Your toddler will probably thread a random pattern, but as he gets older encourage him to follow a pattern such as red, yellow, blue, red, yellow, blue. This activity promotes coordination and fine motor skills. At the end you could tie it into a necklace – but be sensible about leaving your child with string.

BOX CLEVER

Always put aside big cardboard boxes – the sort that washing machines or computers are delivered in. There are so many things to make with big boxes. Make a 'sit-in' train by putting a range of boxes together, adding paper plate wheels and a toilet roll funnel. It could also become an aeroplane or a boat with a few additions. Garages, dolls' houses, rockets, robots and riding stables can also be made with boxes, tubes and some imagination.

THE WORLD'S BEST PLAYTIME DOUGH RECIPE

Another absolute essential for all busy mums is a good playtime dough recipe. For children from around 18 months, making models and patterns with play dough can make a rainy afternoon fly by, so here's Nanny's tried (and much tested!) best recipe:

What you need:

   1 cup of plain flour

   Half a cup of salt

   1 cup of water and colouring (food colouring or powder poster paint)

1 tablespoon cooking oil
2 tablespoons baking powder

What you do: Stir the ingredients together over a low heat until they form a soft ball. Cool and store in the fridge in a plastic sealable box.

Gloop

Cornflour makes another unexpected playtime 'dough'. Nanny has been using this for years and it never fails to mesmerise babies and toddlers. Mix the cornflour with a little water to produce a 'gloop' that changes shape and moves, as if by magic. It's worth stripping your little one down to his nappy and vest – that way he's free to play and he'll love the sensation of 'gloop' trickling on to his hands, legs and tummy. Protect the surrounding area with a sheet of plastic as it can get messy, but rest assured it does wash out.

PLAY DETECTIVES – SECRET WRITING

This is a great one for you to enjoy with an older child.

What you need: *Lemon juice, Fine paintbrush, Paper, Lamp or torch*
What you do: Dip the paintbrush into the lemon juice and write your message on the paper. Wait for the paper to dry. When it is dry you will not be able to see it – but hold it up to a lamp and what do you see? The secret message!

MINI MATHEMATICIANS AND SUPER SCIENTISTS

Children love to find out how things work and how to make them work. You can encourage this by collecting a range of plastic measuring jugs and bowls and letting your child measure and fill up containers with water to different levels. Always show and ask – for example, show your child where the litre or pint level is on a measuring jug and ask him to fill the jug to that level and pour it into another container.

Big Foot

Take some card or paper and draw round everyone's feet. If you
want to get really messy you could do this by creating paint footprints using poster paint and a tray, but it is best done outside on
a sunny day. Once you have about eight footprints (don't forget
friends' and the dog's), measure them with a ruler. Who has the
biggest? Who has the smallest? Who has the widest? Who has the
biggest big toe? If you keep the footprints you can see how much
everyone has grown when you play again next year.

3-2-1 Take Off!

One of Nanny's favourite science projects is making things that
go pop. You can make a great rocket launcher using stuff you have
in your kitchen.

What you need: Paper plate, cardboard toilet tube, felt pens, white
vinegar, baking soda and an old plastic film container. In the age
of digital cameras, getting an old plastic film container may be a
problem but ask older relatives (white canisters are best)

What you do: Cover the tube with white paper and fasten it with
tape or child-friendly glue. Tape the tube to the centre of the
plate. You and your child can decorate the tube and plate
with stripes, stars, numbers or names. This will be the launch
pad. Check out pictures of rockets on the NASA website for
inspiration. The film container will be placed inside the tube –
but it's only the lid that will be rocketing skyward. Your launch
pad and container base stay firmly on the ground. You now need
to place this launcher outside and put rocket fuel in your roar-
ing rocket (the film container). An adult needs to be ground
control for this part of the launch. Place the film container near
the launcher but not inside yet. Put 1 tablespoon of vinegar in
the film container and add half a teaspoon of baking soda. As
quickly as you can, put the lid on and place it upright in the
cardboard tube.

STAND WELL BACK. You and your budding rocket scientist can do the countdown. It will usually launch after about 10–15 seconds. The lid will fire into the air, sometimes to about 3 metres. If it doesn't launch, wait for a further minute before approaching it and tip the launcher over so that if the lid does fire off, it doesn't hit you. It won't hurt as it's only small and baking powder is safe, but it will make you jump and could be mildly unpleasant if it hits your eye.

MAKING MUSIC

Nanny makes music part of everyday life, from the soothing tunes she plays to her charges as babies, to nursery rhymes and fun songs that get them bouncing around. From an early age, children will enjoy listening to all sorts of music, in the car, on the radio, during play. Music doesn't just make you all feel good; for children it can also help with many areas of development. Nanny uses music in the following ways:

- **Language and listening:** from nursery rhymes to clapping songs, music helps your child to remember words and listen.
- **Feelings and emotions:** music is designed to create a mood – sad or upbeat, sombre or frenetic. Movement to music can encourage self-expression.
- **Rhythm:** clapping along to nursery rhymes and tunes helps your child understand rhythm and beat.
- **Movement and exercise:** dance and movement to music help children burn off energy.

Nanny knows a range of fun musical games and activities that will encourage your little prodigy to love music:

Be a Musical Explorer

Play many different musical styles – from rock to Baroque – to your child, not just children's songs. You can encourage your child to listen and imagine by playing a piece of classical music and asking him to describe what he hears. Does the music sound like wind in the trees? Does it sound like birds? What colours does he think of when he listens and why? You can use music to encourage an understanding of emotions by asking questions such as, is the music happy or sad, busy or lazy, loud or soft? You can clap the rhythm along with the music and ask if it is fast or slow. There are many classical CDs of music composed with children in mind – try Prokofiev's *Peter and the Wolf* or Saint-Saëns' *Carnival of the Animals*.

NANNY'S TOP TIP
Use music to change the mood at home or in the car, and to signal calm down time if things are getting too raucous.

Strictly Go Dancing

Another fun game is to put on a piece of music and dance around the room with your child. It's a great feeling just to let go and it's good exercise – and remember no one is watching so you can dance as badly as you like. You could make it more interesting by doing actions to the music. Pretend you are horses and trot around the room or put some rock music on and play air guitar and jump about. Anything goes in the world of dance and music, so just let your twinkle toes run riot.

Pot and Pan Orchestra

If you want some noisy fun don't forget that you have the makings of an orchestra in your kitchen cupboards, so get out pots and pans, lids and wooden spoons, and fill plastic containers with buttons or beads. The pans and spoons are drums, the pan lids are cymbals, and the tub of beads is a maraca. Put on some music or use a nursery song such as 'I am a music man, I come from down your way ...' If you don't know it, you can find the words and music on the internet. The neighbours may need some earplugs, but your little virtuoso will love it.

Live Music
Introduce your child to live music. Watch buskers when you are out shopping; take him to an outdoor concert or festival. Outdoor concerts are best for young children as they are much easier to leave if your child gets bored or hungry. If he is still in his pushchair, take it along as he can watch or fall asleep.

The Great Outdoors

Nanny knows how important it is for children to have fresh air, but the great outdoors – be it a park, a garden, woodland or the seaside – is more than just a great place for children to burn off energy. Children learn through active play and exploring, and discovering their surroundings is an important part of their development. A bit of risk is important too, such as climbing trees or making camp fires. Remember, Nanny is not afraid of weather; she takes the children to play outside come rain or shine. Splashing in puddles, kicking leaves and throwing snowballs is all fantastic fun for your child, as long as he has suitable clothing.

TURN OFF YOUR MOBILE PHONE
How many times have you sat in the park and watched all the mummies sitting with mobile phones glued to their ears while their ignored tots play? Norland Nannies are not allowed to be

seen in uniform using a mobile phone; the reason is that when they are working, the child's welfare is paramount. So make sure that when you have time in the park together you use it to play with your child, or watch him play with others – a joy in itself. Your child is not safe if you are distracted, gossiping with a girl-friend on your mobile or texting your work schedule to a colleague. There's also a more important reason. All children like to show off to their parents and get their approval: 'Look Mummy, look what I can do!' is a phrase we all hear from our children, and that's because they want to know that you are watching them swing, run and climb.

Learn from your child by watching him play. It is a wonderful experience and a relaxing time for you, so make the most of it. You will discover how your child interacts with other children, how he copes with problems and how happy playtime can make him. Childcare professionals are trained to observe children at play; it is a great thing for parents to do too because you can spot small achievements or difficulties. Your child will love this un-divided attention.

RUN WILD

A child who has burnt off energy running around a park will be happier, sleep better, eat better, and his general fitness and muscle strength will improve. With younger babies, let them have a kick on a changing mat under the trees shaded from the sunshine without a nappy. Allow your toddler to walk with you and not always have to sit in the buggy. Take your child swim-ming – you can start this from around six weeks old, once he has had all his immunisations. Physical play helps with key skills such as hand–eye coordination, and it can even help self-esteem and independence. By playing outside, your child will also begin to understand risk, so let him climb trees and play hide and seek.

Green Means Go!

The traffic light game is a great variation on musical statues. It's a good one to play if you have met up with other families in the park. Find an open space and explain to the children what each colour means: red means stop, amber means get ready, green means go. Everyone pretends to drive a car or bus, ride a bicycle or motorbike, doing the actions and making the sounds. When you shout that the light is green, everyone roars around; shout amber and they slow down ... and on red everyone stops, absolutely still, no moving. Repeat ... endlessly! With older children, adapt the game so that if they move when the light is red, they have to spend the next go in the police pound. They are only released when the next person is caught for jumping a light – or speeding!

Teddy Bears' Picnic

This is a winner with small children in the garden or the park. Select favourite teddies and meet up with some friends to lay on a teddy bears' picnic. One, two, three: 'If you go down to the woods today you're sure of a big surprise ...'

NANNY'S TOP TIP

Use inexpensive crockery for your picnics, not plastic children's sets. This encourages responsibility and care with the household china.

Be a Nature Explorer ...

Junior explorers travel to jungles and deserts and unknown territory, and your garden or the local park can become the Antarctic or the Amazon jungle with some imagination. Put together an explorer's outfit: a sun hat, a rucksack, shorts and walking boots. Have an explorer's kit in a bag – include a pair of old (not valuable) binoculars, a notebook and pencil, a bug box (plastic tub) for collecting small creatures and a magnifying glass. Go in search of wild animals to identify. Guides to woodlice, insects and other small creatures can be downloaded from the web.

If your child (or you) isn't keen on creepy crawlies, search for objects such as leaves, bark, twigs, feathers and conkers. Get your child to feel the texture of each natural treasure. Make sure that once your child has examined his finds, any animals are returned to where you found them. If you have to take bugs home, encourage your child to care of them for a few days and then return them. Nanny knows of many tadpoles that have met an untimely end after a few days left in a jam jar.

If you don't fancy being explorers, be natural artists. Collect twigs, sticks, leaves and acorns and make a nature sculpture, fort or fairy house. It's a perfect pastime for the beach, a woodland, park or garden.

Tents and Teepees

On a warm day construct a shelter or tent. You can make one by pegging two old sheets over the washing line and securing the bottoms with some stones. For a small child, a den can be anything from a piece of netting hung from a branch to some sheets over a picnic table. Children love secret spaces, so a den is a great way of giving them their own hidey-hole where they know they can have adventures, be on their own or read a book. So make it a special place with cushions, a plastic tub or tin of snacks and torches. Ready-made children's tents, beach shelters and dens can be bought from the shops, but often it's more fun making your own. Here's how to make a very basic teepee:

'**My Space' Teepee**: Take three or four long bamboo poles and strap together at the top by rope or parcel tape. The bases need to stick into the ground. Drape a large piece of material or old sheet around and fix using clothes pegs. This makes an ideal wigwam for one small child.

Nanny recommends that parents and carers have a 'den box' in the garage or attic. Collect old sheets, beach mats, blankets and table cloths, which can be pulled out on sunny days to create a temporary shelter.

Feed the Birds

Children love watching animals – a simple bird feeder or bird table in the garden or on your windowsill can attract birds and squirrels. Make a bird cake by melting some lard or vegetable fat in a pan and adding nuts and seeds. Pour into a plastic tub (the sort you get cottage cheese or dips in) and allow to set. When set, make a hole through the 'cake' and the container using a knitting needle or similar implement, and thread a piece of string through and knot. Hang the container with the cake upside down on a bird table or tree. It should attract finches, tits and robins. Make a list of all the different birds that visit each day. This is an excellent way to have some quiet time together on a rainy day as you can still watch through a nearby window.

Every Cloud has a Silver Lining ...

You can transform a rainy day from a damp squib to a fun day together by starting a project on the weather. Help a toddler to measure rainfall by putting a plastic pot or measuring jug out in the rain to see how much water falls. Make a flag and hang it from the washing line, and with a compass work out the direction of the wind. Collect fir cones from a woodland walk and watch them open and close depending on the temperature. Record all your findings in a notebook. This could become a bigger project on the weather if your child is interested. You could make paper snowflakes, paint pictures of your garden or park in different weathers, or make seasonal collages.

MAKING A MESS

Children are used to being told not to get dirty, so when mum or dad lets them make a big mess, it's a joy not to be missed. The best way to keep your sanity and your furnishings splatter-free is to do these activities outside.

Home-made Beach

You can buy ready-made sand pits, but with young children any plastic container of sand will do, even an old washing-up bowl or baby bath. Transform the sand pit into a beach by adding seashells, water, toy boats, buckets and spades. Wear sun hats and sunglasses, even if the day is overcast – and don't forget to supply some ice creams. Alternatively, you can make it a building site with cars and trucks. A sandpit is a good permanent plaything to have, but always cover it at night as it attracts the local cats.

Action Art

Get some large pieces of paper such as rolls of lining paper or wallpaper. Use masking tape to attach a long section to a flat piece of ground like a patio or lawn – somewhere you can hose down afterwards. You will need big plastic trays or tubs for lots of poster paint, and make sure the paint is washable. Old swimming costumes or shorts are the outfits Nanny recommends. The children dip their feet in the paint and walk, hop or run across the paper.

There's no doubt the children will love the mess, but you might not. So here's Nanny's checklist for keeping the mess manageable – well almost …

Nanny's Minimal Mess Checklist:
- It's going to get messy so relax – it's only paint!
- Put down plastic sheets.
- Use old clothes or aprons – or if it's warm, let the children go naked.
- Messy play outside is best, but if you are prepared you can do it indoors – the kitchen is probably best as it usually has a wipeable floor.

Play that Prepares for School

At school, your child will need to be able to sit still, be attentive, concentrate, make friends and be in a crowd without mum or dad. He will need to control his pencil and be able to communicate well. You can help your child by playing games that will help him adjust to school life. Playing the Traffic Light Game (see page 207) or other games described earlier in this chapter or reading stories together will help him develop listening skills. Games in the great outdoors such as finding insects and small animals, or looking for different textures or shapes in nature will encourage him to observe his world. Talking to your child as you play and encouraging him to answer will help him with his language and communication skills, and being able to communicate with his friends and his teacher will be a great advantage in his early school years. If you have allowed your child to develop at his own pace, encouraged by creative and imaginative play, he will come to understand the world and his own place in it.

CHAPTER 7
party nanny

Norland Nannies have attended and organised thousands of children's parties, so in this chapter, Nanny gives you a step-by-step guide to creating the perfect party. With a selection of favourite games, party themes and menus to give you a head start, you can throw an enchanting party for your child to remember forever.

Parents often compete for 'best children's party', but remember parties just have to be fun. The simplest parties are frequently the most enjoyable because young children have no idea what anything costs, and as the parent you are not under any pressure to perform.

Let's Start at the Very Beginning ...

First you need to decide on a theme for the party. The best way to do this is to ask the birthday boy or girl what he or she would like. You can almost guarantee they will decide on the one theme you fear making the most, but there are ways to accommodate your child's wishes, however artistically challenged you are. There are three ways to approach a themed party:

- Buy everything from a specialist party shop – not Nanny's favourite option.
- Buy some bits and pieces and enjoy putting party bags together – okay, but still not as much fun as Nanny would like.
- Design and make everything yourself with books to help you, being sure to keep it simple – this gets a Nanny thumbs-up.

Super-busy parents may blanch at the thought of making everything from scratch, but if you plan far enough in advance and have realistic goals, you and your little party animal can have some creative fun.

Depending on your child's age, you may need to guide him in the choice of theme and how much the two of you can achieve before the big day. Age-appropriate parties give everyone the most fun – which does not include the parents. Nanny has attended her share of champagne and canapé parties for two-year-olds, and the toddlers did not enjoy them much.

PIRATES (FOR TODDLERS UPWARDS)

Everything is based around the Jolly Roger and birthday boy is the captain (if he wants to be). Outdoor games might be walking the plank (a wide plank of wood balanced between two low upturned buckets), or a Treasure Island hunt complete with treasure map photocopied for every child. Indoor creative time with black paper, string and scissors means everyone makes their own eye-patch. You can pop chocolate gold coins into your party bags.

OUTER SPACE (BETTER FOR YOUNG SCHOOL CHILDREN)

Pretend your house or garden is the Moon or Mars. Make all your games space themed, so musical chairs becomes musical planets; treasure hunts are for silver-wrapped chocolate stars and small space rocket toys. Revamp a simple game of tag to get some run-around time outside. Everyone chooses the name of a planet and the child who is 'it' is a meteor. When the meteor tags a planet, he assumes the planet's name and the ex-planet is the new meteor. For the party tea, juices become rocket fuel and biscuits are star shaped. It can be fancy dress if you like. Let your imagination run where no mum or dad has gone before!

ACTIVITY PARTIES

Older children may choose a swimming, archery or go-karting party, but smaller children can have activity parties too. Indoors, toddlers can paint, glue and stick; an old baby's bath tub can be filled with cornflour mixture (see Chapter 6, page 201 for a recipe) and wooden spoons, plastic bowls and jugs provided for toddlers to measure and pour. If you have enough room, you can build a mini assault course with cushions, laundry baskets and cardboard boxes – toddlers will have lots of fun following the course.

WINTER FOREST PARTY

If you have a winter child, you don't have to shun the great outdoors. Nanny is a great advocate of fresh air for healthy children – whatever the weather. You can have a Winter Forest Party in your garden or in an open green space if you prefer. It is brilliant fun for all age ranges from two years upwards. Toddlers need quite a bit of supervision – probably one adult to every two children. You can organise them collecting sticks to make a fire; they can go bug hunting and leaf collecting. With adult help, toddlers can make dens and bring their teddies with them to join in. You can even play hunt the teddy bear. A forest party is all about smell and touch – toddlers can smell leaves and earth and tell you what they think; they can be asked to find something rough, something smooth, something round.

When it comes to forest tea parties, once an adult has got the fire burning, the children can hold marshmallows over the fire on long sticks. They will love hearing popcorn go bang inside a can over the fire, and they can even wrap their own potatoes in foil to roast in the embers, but they will need help taking them out and cutting them open to cool down.

NANNY'S TOP TIP

Remove hot marshmallows from a stick with two rich tea biscuits. Hold one either side of the marshmallow and pull it off the stick, then you can squash the marshmallow into a sandwich for it to cool and no one's fingers will come into contact with a super-heated sweetie.

The forest party can work for all seasons and all ages. Just take the basics and let your imagination do the rest.

BONFIRE PARTY

Anyone can enjoy a bonfire but for it to work best, this is probably one for older children. They can gather the wood for the fire; they can learn how to build a bonfire to make it light first time and one of them can be responsible for lighting it under adult supervision. Jacket potatoes in foil are good fun, and if you get the menu right (see page 217) then the party tea becomes hassle free.

TEDDY BEARS' PICNIC

For the outdoor summer party, this works well with little ones. Everyone brings a teddy so they all have someone to cuddle if it gets too much, and the teddies can join in the fun. Try to organise the children to sit child-teddy-child-teddy. Play Ring-a-Ring of Roses with the children holding teddies between them. Teddy bear hunts and teddy races burn off energy.

Organising a Party

Once your birthday boy or girl has decided on the theme, you should draw up the guest list. Parties for tiny babies are more about celebrating your first year together as a new family than about the child having a memorable time. Once your child starts nursery or school, you may end up with the entire class on the guest list. Remember to guide him depending on the size of your home, the venue you have chosen, your budget or simply your level of patience.

If your child has older or younger siblings, it may help if they invite a friend too. It will give them someone of their own age to play with and they may even be able to help you. So, now you have a guest list and a theme, it's time to create your party.

Nanny's Party Checklist:
- Invitations and RSVPs
- Helpers
- Menu planning
- Birthday cake
- Setting the table
- Party decorations
- Party bags
- Prizes
- Safety check
- Party timetable
- Games

PARTY INVITATIONS AND RSVPS

Party invitations should include your child's name, your address and telephone number and possibly an email address. Parents will need to know what time the party starts and is intended to finish. Do not forget to tell your guests what the theme is, especially if they need to a make a costume. Sometimes guests need some practical guidance on what to wear – such as wellington boots, old clothes or a painting smock, swimming costume and towel – that way nobody ends up disappointed and unable to join in. Keep some spares of your own to hand just in case.

Asking busy parents to reply is a lot easier if you provide your mobile phone number so they can text you. Alternatively, enclose an RSVP slip. Make sure parents inform you of their mobile number, child's allergies or medication, or just plain likes and dislikes, and ask if the parent is staying or not. If you know this, then you can plan how many grandparents, aunts and uncles you need to pressgang into helping you.

HELPERS

For the party to run smoothly and allow you time with the birthday child, you will need a helping hand – a partner, good friend or relative. Give them a specific role and allow them to get on with it, such as organising games and setting out party food.

PARTY MENUS

Party menus should be simple, nutritious and fun. Organise the tea party so that it is at the time your child and his friends normally have lunch or tea. Provide plenty of finger foods and snacks at the table to allow the hungrier children to have their fill while the excited children can pick what they need to keep going. Remember to help each child to lots of drinks – children who have been running around are thirsty even if they do not know it.

You cannot hope to cater for all likes and dislikes, but hopefully your RSVPs will have given you a hint of any 'no go' areas such as allergies or special diets. If you have guests with special requirements, then tailor the menu towards them. Avoid providing a separate meal since this might make the child feel different and isolated.

Here are three sample party menus including one for lactose-intolerant guests:

Pirate Menu

- **Treasure Island sandwiches:** open sandwiches laid out on a sandy-coloured plate or tray, topped with ham, cheese, tomato and cucumber.

- **Caribbean dip:** equal quantities of cream cheese and plain yoghurt mixed together in a bowl. Add diced ham, pineapple chunks and ground pepper, and mix well.
- **Vegetable batons:** sticks of carrot, cucumber, celery and peppers to dip.
- **Polly Parrot mix:** mix sunflower seeds and diced dried fruit in a bowl (avoid nuts for all ages).
- **Pirate boats:** orange quarters lying on their backs with a cocktail stick and a triangle of white paper for the sail.
- **Pirate punch:** a range of pure fruit juices in a punch bowl. Add the fizz from sparkling water (not fizzy pop).
- **Cannon balls:** roll cake crumbs and digestive biscuit crumbs in cocoa powder in a bowl. Add honey (for the over twos) and a tiny dash of rum essence. Mix into a stiff paste and pat into balls in your hands. Now pour vermicelli chocolate strands into a shallow bowl and roll the balls around until covered. Serve them in piled mounds ready to fire.

Bonfire Buffet

This menu is hassle-free for the parents and lots of fun for slightly older children. Lay out the basics on a trestle table for the children to help themselves.

- **Hamburgers and hotdogs:** lots of buns sliced in two. Hamburgers and sausages can be cooked over the fire (supervise to make sure they are well cooked). Provide lots of relishes and dishes of sliced tomato and cucumber.
- **Soup:** serve soups in polystyrene cups and wrap a napkin round them to protect hands. Sweetcorn chowder or tomato soup are frosty evening favourites.

- **Mulled punch:** they will think they are so grown up! Mix orange juice and blackcurrant cordial in a large punch bowl, add a teaspoon of cinnamon, boiling water to dilute and rounds of thinly sliced oranges to float on top (check temperature before serving).
- **Puddings:** flapjacks and caramel squares are easily eaten from gloved hands, and toffee apples on a stick are bonfire favourites.

Alternative for Lactose-intolerant Guests

- **Pizza:** make your own base using a basic scone dough and replace butter with dairy-free margarine, and milk with water. Now you can top the pizza with lots of fresh ingredients and a homemade tomato sauce. Miss out the cheese and put a dish of grated cheese to one side for little fingers to help themselves.
- **Hummus dip with vegetable batons:** celery, carrot, peppers, raw broccoli florets, cucumber.
- **Fresh lemonade:** this will impress the children and the parents, and is packed full of vitamin C.

THE BIRTHDAY CAKE

The Swiss roll is the best friend of every parent whose child has grand and fanciful designs for a birthday cake. Armed with a Swiss roll or two, Nanny has conjured up steam trains, mermaids, owls and robots – the list is endless. Nanny makes her own Swiss roll, but busy parents can buy them in any supermarket. Here are three of Nanny's timeless favourite cake designs to whet your appetite:

Steam Train

A long cylinder of Swiss roll forms the train's body with carved squares of Swiss roll for the cab. Rounds of trimmed Swiss roll are the wheels – three on each side. Cover the train in blue icing and pipe red icing along its flanks. The piston rods connecting the wheels can be liquorice bootlaces; a yellow Liquorice Allsort is the dome and a black one is the funnel. Use one of your child's picture books as inspiration.

Old MacDonald's Farm

Bake a large, deep, square Victoria sponge. Cover it with chocolate icing and make a fence round it using chocolate fingers pushed into the sponge. Now you can put plastic tractors and animals in the middle along with the candles.

Rock Pool Cake

A round Victoria sponge is the basis for a rock pool cake. The sponge is covered in blue icing on all sides. Cut red, orange and green icing into triangular fish shapes, octopus, seaweed and even a diver or two to decorate the sides. Put a plastic boat sailing alone on top. Candles round the outside mark the edge of the known world.

NANNY'S TOP TIP

If you have twins or triplets, you may end up with a conflict of party interests – they may not like the same things. If this happens, Nanny has a suggestion: have two parties on separate days. After all, your twins or triplets are individuals, so let their personalities shine through in their choice of party activities and guests.

SETTING THE TABLE

Norland Nannies have attended parties where the best china has been used, and parties where no cutlery or crockery has been provided. Nanny recommends paper plates and cups and plastic cutlery. There are no breakages and washing up. Leftover plates are readily turned into face masks if you need an extra party game. Plastic cutlery cannot become a weapon for the excited child.

Paper tablecloths are an obvious solution to party mess – they protect the table from mishaps and turn into carry sacks for all the leftovers. All that's required is one swoop with both arms and a quick trip to the dustbin. A plastic sheet under a paper cloth will protect a special dining table. For smaller children, a plastic sheet or newspaper under the table will protect carpets from spills from beakers. Ensure the table covering is short enough to avoid trip hazards. Having no cloth may work with a table that is easily wiped clean and is probably the better option with very young children.

NANNY'S TOP TIP

For tear-free refreshments, ask toddlers to bring their own beakers – that way, there's one cup for everyone and they can identify their own.

When it comes to getting everyone to the table, toddlers and pre-schoolers prefer free-form seating arrangements. Avoid a knee-high war and let everyone choose where they sit.

PARTY DECORATIONS

Not every child likes loud noises. The younger your guests, the less likely they are to tolerate surprise bangs. Hence, Nanny never puts party poppers on the tea table or in gift bags – they are dangerous in the hands of excited revellers. Party blowers for slightly older children are a nice idea because they can decide when to blow them.

Party hats are a firm favourite for every age. You and your child can make them together before the party – time and artistic skills permitting – or you can provide a basic hat for each guest and have fun decorating them as a group.

The simplest party hat is a strip of card long enough to circle the head, securely fastened with sticky tape at the back. Do not use staples because they catch in children's hair. Put the hat in the hands of a four-year-old armed with glue and scissors and shapes to cut out, and you have an occupied and creative child. Hat making can form part of your party activities – it is a good distraction and calming activity for the guests to play on a blanket on the floor while you put out food for the tea party.

NANNY'S TOP TIP

Don't turn hat decorating into a competition to be judged by an adult or the birthday child. Children are normally too excited at parties to control their emotions, and any disappointment could cause a downpour.

PARTY BAGS

Most parties end with giving out party bags. All you need are paper bags full of tiny fun gifts as a memento of your child's party. You have chosen your party theme together, which has provided you with lots of creative ideas for invitations, party hats and a cake. For the fully branded birthday party, carry this through to the party bag.

The party bag does not need to be a gift bag. Instead, decorate some plain recyclable paper bags. The basic ingredients are a piece of birthday cake wrapped in a napkin with an inflated balloon (a flat balloon is a choking hazard). However, most party bags are a little more elaborate. Remember to keep party bags age appropriate, and putting in a few intriguing little goodies is more interesting than one or two larger items – tiny fingers love to delve into a bag to find things lurking at the bottom.

Depending on your budget and theme, here are a few ideas to get you started:

- **Nature party bag:** small wildlife picture book, non-sharpened pencil, packet of raisins, piece of cake
- **Forest party bag:** I-spy book of animals, animal badge, items made during the forest party such as leaf collages, piece of forest cake
- **Fairies party bag:** tube of star glitter, small pack of fairy-themed pencils (unsharpened), pink writing pad, fairy hair bobbles, small fairy cakes

Setting yourself a budget for each bag is probably the safest way to keep costs in line with your imagination. Shop around in unusual places like traditional hardware stores and art suppliers, or a cookery shop for cheap imaginative fridge magnets. Remember, children will count everything in their bag and compare it with other guests – so beware the advanced three-year-old mathematician.

PRIZES

Nanny does not provide prizes for children's party games. The exception is pass the parcel, which would never work without a sweetie being found every time a layer is removed. Offer stickers to the last one standing in musical statues or the first across the line in an egg and spoon race. A treasure hunt is a good way to encourage children to seek hidden goodies – everyone stands a chance.

If you cannot bear a party without prizes, then go for quantity and keep them small and different – a selection of dinosaur and fairy badges for older children, and stickers for younger children.

SAFETY CHECK

For Norland Nannies safety comes first. They are trained to take a quick sweep round any party venue. It is only fair to other parents that you take a look at your own home prior to throwing a party. See Chapter 3 for guidance on safety around the home and garden.

Nanny's Sunshine Party Checklist:

- On the invitations ask everyone to bring their own sun cream
- Provide water on tap for children to help themselves
- Make sure the children wear sun hats
- Create a shady 'time-out' area

For winter parties, let everyone know on the invitation to wear coats, hats and scarves and to bring wellington boots.

PARTY TIMETABLE

Your child's age will determine the length and complexity of the party. Toddlers can manage only an hour or two; pre-schoolers can remain pleasantly excited for around two hours before they become tired and grumpy; and older children might make three hours. Then you have to consider how long your patience will last.

NANNY'S TOP TIP

Organise your most active games for the start of the party while everyone is full of bounce.

Guests seldom arrive all together, so the first 10 minutes of your party involve getting everyone in, coats off and briefed. You are marshalling a group of very excited young children who will have more fun if they know where the boundaries are. As you near the birthday tea, organise a quiet game to allow everyone to take a breather.

After tea, you now have a group of children full of juice and cake so keep party games calmer until everyone's tea has had time to settle. 'Pin the tail on the donkey' or 'pin the eye patch on the pirate' are good post-tea games; they keep the children together as a group so they are easily called out to meet their parents and collect their party bag – and hopefully to say thank you.

I once gave a party for a group of boisterous six-year-old boys. They were super-excited and burned through games rapidly. I didn't want anyone to get bored and start making trouble, so I'd organised far more games than I ever imagined I'd need. They nearly ran me dry of new ideas, but I still had a couple left up my sleeve at the end. **Nanny Maria**

If you are having a party entertainer, feel free to give him a list of your child's favourite games. After all, whose party is it? Remember to keep reading the mood of the guests – they might like some free play time every now and then.

PARTY GAMES

Musical statues, musical chairs and treasure hunts are party staples, but Nanny has a few personal party favourites to offer:

Changing Stations (for five-year-olds and upwards)

Blindfold your chosen person and put them in the middle of the room. Each child picks a station name, real or imagined – St Pancras, Paddington, platform 9¾ King's Cross. The parent calls out two names: 'Train travelling from St Pancras to Paris', and the named children swap seats, trying to avoid capture by the blindfolded person. Chaos ensues when the parent shouts 'All change'. If you are caught, it is your turn to wear the blindfold.

Pass the Balloon

This can be played both indoors and outdoors and requires a few inflated balloons. Ask the children to split into teams. Now they can pass the balloon along the row of children in their team; the winning team is the one to get to the end first. The complexity of the game depends on age and ability – you can pass the balloon using hands, knees or just heads. This gets lots of laughs and gets the children working together.

One Finger One Thumb

This is a good post-tea party song game for all ages and ideal for giving everyone a rest while keeping their jelly and juice down. It encourages children to sit quietly at the beginning while you all sing 'one finger one thumb keep moving, one finger one thumb keep moving, one finger one thumb keep moving and we'll all be merry and bright'. The children can do the actions, wiggling finger and thumb. By the time you have reached 'one finger one thumb one arm one leg one nod of the head stand up turn around sit down keep moving', everyone's party tea should have settled sufficiently for them to be raring to go again. It takes approximately three to five minutes to work your way up to a frenzy.

For any game, the referee's decision is final. Most two- to five-year-olds will not think to question the decision of an adult while playing, but older children may. Do not argue back, but be prepared to move quickly on to the next game to divert attention – renewed excitement will usually defuse any brewing animosity.

Not all children will be equally confident at the start of a party, so remember to watch out for the child who is struggling to join in. A shy child may benefit from their parent staying until they are settled into the games, or ask an older child to buddy them. If it is not working out, at least you have the parent's phone number from their RSVP so you can call for emergency backup.

At the end of a party, the well-mannered party-goer never forgets to say thank you to the birthday child's mummy, and she never forgets to help her child write thank you notes for all his presents. If good behaviour has been lacking at this year's party, Nanny has some no-nonsense advice to ensure better behaviour from everyone next year in the following chapter.

CHAPTER 8
no-nonsense nanny

No nonsense … it may sound as if Nanny is harking back to those stiff and starched Victorian matrons who instilled rules with a rod of iron, and whose charges were seen and not heard. She's not. Discipline is not smacking; it is not threatening; it is not being horrid. It is about guiding your child to do the right thing; his values, his morals and his social skills are learnt from you and those he is in close contact with. What does that mean? Well, it means that this chapter is primarily about *you* – not your child. If you know how to be a well-behaved parent and deal with bad behaviour effectively, life's little childhood challenges will be less of a problem. Nanny will help *you* instil discipline by transforming your language, your approach and your ability to handle challenging behaviour. As ever, though, she is realistic – even the best parents with the most angelic children still occasionally experience tantrums and other toddler trademarks. So this chapter will also suggest some simple strategies for helping you and your child through those difficult moments, if they do happen.

Well-behaved Parents

Throughout life we are taught how to do things – how to ride a bike, how to drive a car, how to swim – but no one teaches us how to be parents. We learn much of what we do from our own parents, and unfortunately they are not always the best teachers. The way to bring up a happy and well-behaved child is for parents or carers to set clear boundaries. A good parent needs to be **firm but fair**, be **consistent,** set **ground rules** and stick to them.

This view is not based just on Nanny's long experience; it is backed up by child psychologists and paediatricians. Recent research in the UK indicates that children who are brought up by adults who impose non-negotiable boundaries and who use a combination of affection and discipline are more likely to develop self-control, empathy and responsibility for themselves and others. Learning this self-control and self-reliance is an essential part of growing up.

Children, no matter how relaxed or strict their upbringing, have to learn how to deal with frustration, anger, jealousy and all the other emotions that make them human. It is how parents respond that will help guide them. This isn't suggesting a return to strict, unbending parenting, but it is advocating an approach where you articulate to your child where the limits are set and what the consequences are should rules be broken.

Being a firm but fair parent may seem like a big and terrifying responsibility, but Nanny has a straightforward approach:

Nanny's 'Five Bs' for Good Parenting:
- **Be encouraging and positive**. Your child loves to see you happy and smiling. If you give praise and a hug when he has behaved well, he is more likely to remember to be good. It works much better than telling him when he has done something wrong.
- **Be an example**. It may not seem like it, but your child wants to be like you and do what you do. So hearing you say thank you or sorry, or seeing you help an old lady at the shops sets an example.
- **Be firm**. Children need guidelines. Set ground rules (such as on bedtime, amount of time on the computer) and stick to them.

- **Be consistent**. Make sure that everyone involved in caring for your child (nanny, childminder, granny) is saying the same thing day after day. If you say one thing and daddy says the opposite, it will take longer for your child to learn what is right.
- **Be yourself**. Know what is right for you and your child, and forget about what other parents are saying works for their children or what stage they are at. Parenthood is not a competition.

Plain Talking

One of the most important ways to put into action a positive approach to parenting is to think about how you talk to your child. All education is based on language, and this is one of the most important skills that a parent can encourage. Using the right language does take patience and practice on your part. Children don't have to be able to respond for them to understand what you're saying, so continue to speak as an adult, normally and politely. Comments such as 'Thank you for helping me tidy up your toys. Mummy really liked that' or 'That was very kind to let Sarah play with your train set' help your child understand when they have behaved well. This approach will also encourage your child to respond positively, using similar phrases, and it will help him to be more cooperative. If you can both explain when things are going right – or wrong – it means your child is much less likely to become frustrated.

NANNY'S TOP TIP

Avoid baby talk. Use the correct words from day one. This will encourage your child to communicate clearly.

REJECT THE BEHAVIOUR, NOT THE CHILD

This is one of Nanny's golden rules. Rather than saying 'If you bite Tom again I'm going to get angry' or 'Biting is bad, you are very naughty!' reword the sentence: 'Biting hurts. Tom is very upset because you hurt him. How would you feel if Tom bit you?' By wording it this way, you are blaming the behaviour, not blaming the child. With older children, give them the skills to improve their own behaviour with questions such as 'Kicking isn't right. If Tom takes your toy again, can you tell mummy and then we can decide what to do about it together?'

NO

This is a difficult word for many children, so often it is best to give an alternative rather than an outright negative. For example, instead of snapping 'No, you can't have it', try something more reasonable like 'You can't have it now as it's bedtime, but would you like to play with it after breakfast tomorrow?' or 'Having an ice cream is a wonderful idea, but why don't we wait till the weekend when daddy can have one too?'

Explanations work because they help your child to understand the reasons why something can't be done. Having to explain everything can be exhausting for a time-starved, sleep-deprived adult, but if the child knows that you explain, he will use this skill to explain his own emotions rather than losing his temper.

Loving your child doesn't mean letting them have their own way all the time. I always think before I say 'no'. If a child wants to play when he has homework to do, instead of saying 'No, you haven't finished your homework' I always say 'Yes, of course, once you've finished your homework'. **Nanny Sarah**

WHINGEING AND WHINING

This is the one thing that drives most parents to distraction but there are a number of ways you can minimise it. Make sure *you* don't use a whining voice when asking your child to do things. Many parents are unaware that they nag their children in a whining voice and so you need to lead by example. If your child whines, but his request is reasonable, state calmly that of course he can have what he is asking for, but only when he asks for it in a normal voice.

> We used to have a joke about a whinge alert. We would do an impersonation of a police siren whenever Archie whined. By making him laugh when he was whining, he soon understood that it was a bit silly, and so would ask for things in a normal voice. **Nanny Louise**

SHOUTING

This is a waste of energy. Children can drive you mad sometimes, but try not to raise your voice as it can make a situation worse. If your child is in danger, of course you should shout a warning or a command. Sometimes pumping up the volume will be needed to get a child's attention, but don't use it for everyday discipline. If you shout at your child, the chances are he will shout at you. If you shout all the time, it soon has no effect. You can be firm so that your child knows the difference between when you are being fun and when you are being stern, but keep the volume down. Calm is contagious.

> I always lower my voice when dealing with a problem. If a child is shouting he will usually stop to try and listen to you. **Nanny Julia**

THREATS

Parents commonly use threats to reprimand their children. Next time you are out at the shops or on a bus watch how some people use threats as a weapon. Threats and intimidation promise punishment and tend to be of the 'if you don't behave, you're for it!' variety. They are usually followed by the child being dragged away. This is a redundant and ineffective way of dealing with bad behaviour as the child usually carries on regardless.

Avoidance Tactics for Busy Parents

Once you have mastered the techniques of positive communication, you can then develop your repertoire of avoidance tactics. These help you deflect those situations that may trigger a minor 'wobbly' in your child.

INVOLVE YOUR CHILD

With young children, just getting out of the house on time is often a source of stress for parents and their little ones. A young child, particularly a toddler, will be easily distracted and will often become preoccupied with his toys or games just as you want to leave the house. One way to speed up departure is to involve the child in getting ready to go out. Ask questions and set challenges, such as 'Can you get your socks on before mummy has packed her bag?' or 'Can you find your beaker before daddy has made the sandwiches?' The more you can involve your child in the process, the easier it will be.

INTRODUCE CHOICE

One of the main problems for small children is that they have little control over their lives. Parents, carers and grandparents make all the decisions for them, so tantrums and bad behaviour can often be avoided by giving your child a choice. Nanny doesn't mean over the big decisions in his life, like when he goes to bed or if he can watch unlimited television, but the little ones that he can control. Would he like to wear his blue trousers or red ones? Would he like to try the toilet or the potty? Would he like broccoli or carrots?

Be careful not to ask questions that give him the opportunity to say 'no'. If you ask him if he wants to go to grandma's, he might refuse, but if you ask him if he would like to take a cake or some biscuits as a surprise when you visit grandma, it gives him a choice that doesn't affect your decision to visit. Nanny knows that giving a bit of control to your child makes a huge difference and helps him develop self-reliance, allowing him to practise making decisions for himself.

LET HIM DO IT HIMSELF

Nanny always asks children to do things for themselves as soon as they are able. Encourage this from toddler stage by telling your child what a grown-up boy he is when he puts on his own socks or brushes his hair. This will help him to develop independence, confidence and self-esteem. This will help you too, as the earlier a child gets into the habit of laying the table, tidying up his toys or pulling up his duvet, the more likely he is to do it without argument – making mum's life that much easier. How many times do parents complain that they fall out with their children over their untidy bedrooms or that they won't help out at home (especially when they are teenagers)? Introducing age-appropriate tasks around the house will help your child to become more cooperative and helpful, and it shows him that he has an important role to play as part of the family. Nanny knows one family that has relied on their child since the toddler years to get the post when he hears it drop through the letterbox.

REWARDING GOOD BEHAVIOUR

Experts call this 'positive reinforcement' and it works a treat with young children. Nanny only uses this in certain situations, as children need to learn that some things have to be done without question, not just because they will get something out of it. Rewarding your child does not necessarily mean giving toys and sweets; try praise, encouragement and hugs.

Young children love getting stickers and so one of Nanny's favourites for rewarding good behaviour is the sticker chart. If the goal is to get your child to tidy up his toys, clean his teeth or clear the table, he gets a sticker on each day that he has done it and you place it on the chart next to the day of the week. The key to a good chart is to make sure there is something on there that he is good at, as well as something he needs to work at. So if he doesn't always eat his vegetables, but always cleans his teeth, make sure you put both on the chart. Only ask him twice to do the task, as that stops you from nagging and helps the child learn that it is up to him to make the decision to take on the task or not. No task, no sticker. When your child gets a set number of stickers, you show your delight by being over the moon and giving him a treat.

NANNY'S TOP TIP
Sticker charts should only be used for short-term goals – ones that your child can achieve quickly. This stops your child from losing interest.

This is about your child changing his behaviour to win your praise and cuddles, but Nanny wants to be clear here – this isn't just about rewarding your child. It's also about training you to **look for the positive** and praise your child's good behaviour. After all, Nanny loves a well-behaved parent.

Time-out for You

Every member of the family has their own needs. Just because you are a grown-up and a parent it doesn't mean that occasionally you won't experience a tantrum or two yourself. In fact, it's more likely you will have a meltdown because you are a parent! Even the most perfect parent will become tired and run down. Nanny has some good advice for fractious parents too. If you are at boiling point, sometimes it is a good thing to turn away from the situation, go out of the room, or ask someone to watch the children while you have 10 minutes' down-time to calm yourself. Well-behaved adults apologise for their aberrant moments as well.

Occasionally the demands of my own children, after a busy day at work, were just too much. If it happened I would ring grandma or my sister and ask the children to talk to them on the phone. It was a treat for them, and often grandma would read a story down the line. It gave me 10 minutes' breathing space to calm down. **Nanny Maria**

Whatever your child does, remember to keep a sense of humour and perspective. What parents call naughty behaviour is just a normal stage of a child's development. Looking on the sunny side can also help you survive those difficult moments.

Understanding Your Child's Behaviour

Each child is born with his own distinct personality. Where some children will be easygoing and rarely throw a tantrum, others can be more challenging. Tantrums, screaming fits, sulks and answering back are often the childhood challenges parents find most difficult to cope with. It may sound like basic common-sense, but if you understand why your child behaves in certain ways, the more able you will be to manage it.

Difficult behaviour is often part of growing up. It's one way that a child learns what is right, what is wrong, and what he can and can't get away with. After all, one of a baby's first utterances, after 'Daddy' and 'Mummy,' is 'no!' This is the first word in his vocabulary that gives him control over his life. 'No' is just one of many weapons he will use to get a reaction. As he grows, he may add foot stamping, toy throwing and other attention-seeking behaviour to his repertoire. If your child does misbehave, stop and think before you attempt to do anything about it. There is often an event that triggers a meltdown, so before you condemn your little terror to time-out, whisk him off to the health visitor or reach for the gin, ask yourself the following questions:

Nanny's Checklist for Common Causes of Difficult Behaviour:
- Is your baby/child getting enough love and attention?
- Has there been a change in your baby/child's routine?
- Have you been upset or uptight?
- Is your child having a growth spurt?
- Is your child getting enough sleep?
- Is your child getting the right food regularly?

LOVE AND ATTENTION

This may be stating the obvious, but lack of quality attention is often the cause of many behavioural problems. This doesn't mean overindulging your child; just ensure he knows that he is loved. If you can't give him the attention or love he feels he needs, he will start demanding it. A child loves your undivided attention when you read him books, play with him or push him in his buggy. A toddler particularly cannot comprehend why you would not want to be with him all the time. Parents, carers and teachers cannot give a child attention on demand and he will learn this eventually, but it takes a few years to get there. In the interim, he will show his frustration when he doesn't get what he wants. With older children, attention seeking is often a sign that a child feels insecure or has low self-esteem, and children learn very quickly that bad behaviour is a good way of getting their parents or teachers to notice them.

There's no doubt that giving your child the right amount of attention is an exhausting part of parenthood. The solution is simple – give him regular cuddles, tell him that you love him and mean it, and set aside regular times in the day when you play with him or provide an adoring audience to his games. If you cannot be there, make sure he has a routine where he knows when you will be spending quality time with him, reading a story at bedtime or knowing that Saturday morning is time to play football.

ROUTINE

Babies and toddlers like routine. Often an event such as the arrival of a new baby, starting at nursery or crèche, a house move or a holiday can upset this. Even minor routine changes – a toy breaking or starting on the potty – can trigger a wobble. Your child may show his feelings of insecurity by playing up. If you feel change is the cause of difficult behaviour, your goal is to reassure your child and keep his routine as near to normal as possible. If you have introduced something new to his routine, such as potty training, stop and try again in a few days. With toddlers and older children, discuss the changes with them and include them in any decisions. Involving your child in the packing for a holiday or the naming of his new baby sibling will help him feel that he is not being excluded or that his life is irrevocably changing.

YOUR MOOD

Your problems can become your child's problems. Even very young babies have the ability to sense when something is wrong or different and will react when mum or dad is upset, worried or angry. He may not know that you have had a bad day at work or a row with your partner, but he will sense it. This may result in a baby becoming clingy or a toddler having problems staying dry, behaviour guaranteed to make your stress worse.

If you cannot make your problem go away, make sure you provide more comfort and love for your little one than normal. With an older child, you could explain why you are not happy and ask him to help you with something to help you both relax. He then learns empathy and emotional maturity, which enables him to understand that adults (as well as children) are not always happy.

GROWING PAINS

All children go through rapid growth periods. These aren't gradual but tend to come in short bursts. It's not surprising that these can result in a child being irritable or behaving differently – after all, his brain is growing and changing too. There is not much you can do but accept that sometimes he's not playing up, he's growing up, and changes in behaviour are part of his development.

TIREDNESS AND HUNGER

A child who is tired or hungry is likely to be moody and difficult. One of the first things to do is check that he is eating regularly and has a healthy balanced diet. If he has been at a friend's house, has he been eating foods he is not used to? (See Chapter 4 for advice on healthy eating.) Make sure you have a range of energy-boosting snacks available throughout the day – a banana can be a healthy quick fix for children over 12 months. Early nights and a strict sleep routine will help too. Don't forget that your own night-time routine may be causing problems. If you are not getting enough sleep, you will be grouchy and emotional, and less likely to deal with the everyday ups and downs of looking after a family.

Breaking Bad Habits

There are some common behaviours, from tantrums to stubborn refusal to get in a car, which all parents need to be able to deal with. Even if you don't experience them with your own children, you will need this inside information when friends arrive to play or relatives bring their badly behaved offspring to stay. Nanny has dealt with every kind of misdemeanour and knows how to tackle them.

TANTRUMS – AND HOW TO STOP THEM

Living with a toddler is often a battle of wills. He is becoming more independent and learning where his – and your – boundaries are. When he reaches about two years old, your toddler can run and climb but doesn't yet have the skills to realise that his behaviour may be undesirable, unsafe or potentially damaging to himself or his surroundings. His brain has not developed to the point where he can comprehend the repercussions of his behaviour or be able to modify it. At two years old, posting sandwiches into the DVD recorder or putting his head through the banisters isn't naughty; it just seems to be the right thing to do at the time.

At this stage, the 'terrible twos' as they are often called, your child is most likely to show his frustration by throwing a tantrum. Parents need to be able to recognise the tantrum triggers. A tantrum is a way that your child seeks attention when he wants something he can't have, wants to show his independence, wants to express himself but can't, or is over-excited or over-stimulated. There are two types of tantrum:

- **Anger tantrums** are about frustration and usually involve stamping, kicking and biting.
- **Distress tantrums** are when the child is frightened and confused, and generally result in crying, sobbing

or him throwing himself on the floor or banging his head repeatedly.

Many parents fuel tantrums by reacting to them, getting angry, being overly sympathetic or giving in. DON'T. The way to defuse a tantrum quickly is to divert and/or ignore it. Distraction is a good technique to use, but it only tends to work in the early stages before the full-blown tantrum has set in. Often you can see trouble coming and quickly distract your child's attention. To do this effectively, you need to practise changing the subject quickly and dramatically. As soon as you spot the danger signs of a potential toddler meltdown, find something really interesting to look at or talk about a completely new topic. 'Wow! Look at that aeroplane right up there in the sky! I think it's flying to America. Where do you think it might be flying to?' Anything that involves the child in a response, a thought or a plan is perfect. With children under three, Nanny cannot emphasise how useful this technique is, as their attention span is often short anyway. If you can come in with an Oscar-winning performance, your child will often forget what he was going to cry about.

If diversion and your acting prowess fail, the next step if the tantrum takes hold is to remain expressionless and ignore it. Carry on as if nothing is happening; after all, he is after your attention, so if you don't give him any, the tantrum may be short lived. However, there are some moments when nothing will stop your child from blowing his top, usually in a public place at the most embarrassing moment. That's when you need to step in:

Nanny's Tantrum-defusing Technique:
- Count to 10 and breathe deeply before you speak to your child.
- Pick him up and cuddle him, but if the tantrum continues put him down.

- Explain he will have a hug if he stops.
- If the tantrum subsides, pick him up, thank him for stopping and distract him. If it doesn't stop, put him down again.
- Never raise your voice or storm off.
- Once it has stopped, don't mention the tantrum again. It's over.

Often the worst tantrums happen when shopping. Who can blame your little one? The lights, noise and colours amount to an assault on the senses and generally he has to sit still while you shop. Boring! Not only will you have a disapproving audience if your child screams the place down, but it's usually the worst kind of temper tantrum because he can see things he can't have. To avoid this, Nanny always plans ahead. Think of a game to play while you shop (see Chapter 6 for the ABC game), keep trips short and involve your child by letting him help. Talk about your trip and what you are looking for.

NANNY'S TOP TIP
Don't buy sweets or let your child eat in the supermarket. It will prevent him expecting treats while shopping and avoid tantrums when he can't have them.

Rest assured that your child will eventually grow out of the tantrum stage – although it may re-emerge in his teens!

AGGRESSIVE BEHAVIOUR – AND HOW TO DEAL WITH IT

You need to make clear to your child that biting, kicking, punching and pinching are totally unacceptable and will not be tolerated. Often aggressive behaviour is caused by frustration, emotional disturbance, boredom or simply abundant energy.

Many parents use 'time-out' when a child has hurt another child or been unkind; it's a commonly used technique that can be effective to separate the warring parties. However, 'time-out' isn't as simple as some childcare gurus would have us believe. Many children don't necessarily have the emotional maturity to know why they have been excluded. They may refuse to sit on their own, wander off or not do as they are told, which can make the situation worse. It needs careful handling and Nanny prefers her own 'cooling off' technique.

Nanny's 'Cooling Off' Technique:

- Accompany the child to a quieter area.
- Explain calmly and quietly why he has been removed.
- Sit quietly beside him while he settles himself.
- Once he is calmer, ask him to explain what has caused the upset.
- Explain to him that his response to it was unacceptable and why.
- If he is sorry, then invite him to join in again. There must be no hard feelings and it's an open invitation.
- If he repeats the behaviour, remove him and start again.

Always smile and let him know that everything has continued as normal and all his bad behaviour has done is stopped him having a nice time. This emphasises what a waste of time being horrid is.

NANNY'S TOP TIP
Maintain eye contact during tricky behaviour by kneeling or crouching down at his level.

It's also worth thinking about what has triggered the destructive or aggressive behaviour. For instance, has your child been having unhealthy sugar-laden food and drink? If so, make sure he has regular healthy snacks. Too much energy or boredom can also be to blame so always build in some daily high-energy play in a garden or park to help your child let off steam.

EXTREME ATTENTION SEEKING – AND HOW TO STOP IT

Children learn very quickly that bad behaviour is a good way of getting their parents or carers to notice them. Breath-holding is an extreme attention-seeking behaviour in younger children. The breath-holding child often learns that this provokes a massive panic response from his parents and immediately turns all the attention to him. Result! There are two types of breath-holding behaviour:

- **Blue spells** are the most common and are when the child gets angry or frustrated and holds his breath. He turns red and begins to go blue around the mouth. The child often passes out or goes limp.
- **Pale spells** are rarer but more frightening for parents as they can be very dramatic – but are not dangerous on their own. They can result from a tantrum, but a fright or a minor accident can also bring one on. The child opens his mouth but cannot catch his breath; he turns white, goes limp, faints and can go stiff. Some children are sick as the grand finale.

If you have a child who uses either of these breath-holding techniques, stay calm. A child – or adult – cannot suffocate by holding his breath. Even if your child faints, his breathing will begin automatically and he will regain consciousness. All you can do is ride it out, but some basic first aid will help. Ensure that he will not hurt himself if he falls, and if he faints place him in the recovery position (see page 141). If he is sick, make sure his head is forward so he doesn't choke.

> I always found that blowing gently on my daughter's face would encourage her to breathe during a blue spell. **Nanny Julia**

Children usually grow out of breath-holding by the time they reach school age, but keep a careful eye on it in case it is a sign of a more serious ailment, such as epilepsy. Check with your GP if you are concerned.

BAD LANGUAGE – AND HOW TO STOP IT

Children often pick up swearing and offensive remarks from television, from adults (including parents) and in the playground. Naughty words get him a reaction from almost everyone – his friends will think it's hilarious and granny will be shocked. Nanny always handles swearing carefully, as she doesn't want to make the words more appealing by letting a child know that using them gets him attention.

So what do you do when your child has just used a word that would make a builder blush? Your first task is to mind your own language. If you do swear, try to find an alternative that isn't so shocking when your child repeats it. Nanny knows one grandfather who says minor swear words backwards if his grandchildren are in earshot – many expletives certainly seem more innocuous that way. If your little parrot has picked up inappropriate words, don't make a big deal of it and explain that 'these are words that you don't use at home'.

It's not just expletives that can shock the vicar or granny. Children at certain ages find anything to do with bottoms and toilets funny as well. If the words are more playground than pub, don't react either by laughing or getting angry; just ignore them – he will grow out of it.

INTERRUPTING – AND HOW TO STOP IT

Parents are often irritated by toddlers interrupting their conversations or answering back. This is classic attention-seeking as children don't want to be left out; they may be bored or feel that they are being ignored. Most parents will have had the 'telephone moment' when, while trying to talk to someone on the phone, their toddler clamps himself to a leg and demands undivided attention. Nanny avoids this by forward planning. Adapt the treasure basket or rainy day box (see Chapter 6) to make a 'telephone box'. This is full of diverting treats such as crayons and notepaper to take down messages, an old mobile or toy phone to have his own conversations, an 'executive toy' such as a bean bag animal or squeezy ball – anything to help him mimic your behaviour while on the phone. This means that if you do need an uninterrupted moment on the phone, he has something novel to absorb him.

> I looked after a toddler who always screamed and clung to mum when she was on the phone so we bought a toy phone with pre-recorded messages – it worked a treat. Sometimes she was so absorbed in her chat that mummy wasn't allowed to interrupt her! **Nanny Lynne**

WON'T! HOW TO PERSUADE YOUR CHILD TO DO SOMETHING HE DOESN'T WANT TO

Often babies and toddlers will go through a phase of not wanting to be strapped into their seat or pram, so how do you avoid the 20 minutes of negotiation that usually result in you getting grumpy and your child in tears? Nanny has some first-class advice for speeding up departure.

When getting in the car or pushchair, make buckling up fun. Pretend you are pilots or astronauts and you're preparing for take-off. Explain to your child that proper pilots and astronauts *always* use seat belts. Another good technique for the car is to take a teddy or doll and get your child to strap their beloved toy into a spare seat; your little one has to strap himself in too, to show Teddy what to do. Always double check he's strapped himself and Teddy in properly.

> Before getting in the car, I always talk non-stop about where we are going, what we are going to see, what we might do when we get there. This keeps my child's mind on other things while I whisk her into her seat and strap her up in the blink of an eye. **Nanny Louise**

If your child is reluctant to leave the house, another technique is to ask him to organise his own things for the car trip and give him a time limit. Show him on the clock how much time he has until departure, talk through his list and tell him where he can find things; then he is occupied for the 10 minutes before you leave. In the last few minutes, give him a countdown warning and encourage him to run through his checklist, and then race him to the car.

It's not just transport that can cause problems. Some children are also stubborn about having their hair washed or brushed. Nanny prevents tears and tantrums by including a child in the selection of the brush or the shampoo, or by turning it into an event or role-play game. Set up a hairdressers to have customers' hair washed and brushed using dolls or teddies, and ending with your child's hair.

NANNY'S TOP TIP

Make hair washing fun by introducing swimming goggles. This stops soap or shampoo getting in a child's eyes. Wash hair while in the bath then by adding a few bath toys – fish, whales, submarines – he can pretend he is a dolphin or a deep sea diver.

BAD MANNERS – AND HOW TO CHANGE THEM

Once upon a time, Nanny made sure no elbow touched a mahogany dining table and all children minded their p's and q's. Good manners are still something that all children should be taught. Chapters 3 and 4 have already covered good table manners, but your child needs good spoken manners and social skills too. The earlier you introduce the habit of saying 'please', 'thank you' and 'excuse me' the better, and you need to develop those manners yourself if you don't already have them.

Even saying 'good morning' and 'hello' to people is an important skill that we need to teach children. It is a common courtesy to say 'hello' – particularly if someone says it to you first – otherwise it is called 'being rude'. In an age when we have terrified children into not speaking to strangers, they can grow up into socially inept adults who cannot or will not deliver basic courtesies. So make sure your child can differentiate between not talking to strangers and being polite.

If you think this is old fashioned, just consider the benefits: good manners are linked with good social skills, and children with them get on better in life. You will also have a better social life – polite, well-behaved children are always invited again.

'Hellos' and 'goodbyes' are lovely to hear from little ones, but my rule is only to acknowledge strangers if I am with the children. **Nanny Emily**

SIBLING RIVALRY – AND HOW TO DEAL WITH IT

Having one child is relatively simple. He has no one to fight with over the chocolate ice cream or train track, and he has his parents' undivided attention. When other children come along, the family home changes. As Nanny knows all too well, brothers and sisters love to squabble, bait and fight as, guess what? It gets them attention! The arrival of a newborn into an established family unit, especially one with toddlers or young children, is a momentous occasion; and for siblings not always a welcome one.

It is very common for toddlers to misbehave when a new baby arrives, as they feel that their parents' affection and love have been transferred to another. To prevent this, Nanny advises that you introduce your other children to the idea of a baby brother or sister as early as possible. At home, include your other children in everything you are doing to prepare for the new arrival. You might show your older child the *in utero* photos of your first scan. Perhaps take your toddler shopping for the new baby's clothes and ask him to choose a few things himself. He might like to clean his old baby car seat for his 'baby sister or brother' – a special job for him since he is now no longer the baby. If you explain what is happening as your pregnancy progresses, your children will feel included and be more cooperative when the new baby brother or sister arrives.

To avoid any jealousy, some childcare experts suggest that the new baby 'buys' a toy for his older siblings, on the day of his arrival. Nanny also recommends that when you are first introducing your new baby to his brother or sister, you put the baby down in his cot and give your older child a massive hug. This will show him that the new addition has not usurped his position and normal 'mummy cuddling service' has been resumed post-labour. Be prepared for the fact that existing young children may need more attention in those first days than their new sibling.

> **NANNY'S TOP TIP**
> If your toddler is ready to go into a big bed, complete this transition before the arrival of a newborn who will be sleeping in his old cot. This avoids any resentment of the new baby invading his 'territory'.

Sibling rivalry is often at its worst between the ages of 4 and 11. No matter what you do as a parent, there will always be jealousy, competitiveness and accusations of parents being unfair or favouring one brother or sister over another. As a parent you will be negotiating peace deals on a regular basis. Nanny's only advice here is that you'll have to live with it. Use the techniques outlined in this chapter if they fight or quarrel, and rest assured they may grow out of it by the time they are 18 – possibly.

When Every Day is a Bad Day

Sometimes all the good parenting and advice in the world makes no difference to a child's behaviour. Children who are persistently restless, unable to concentrate, destructive, irritable and aggressive may have an underlying condition that they just can't help. The common ones are:

- **Autism and Asperger syndrome:** may lead to problems in understanding and using language.

- **Hearing problems:** deafness and glue ear can make it hard for a child to follow instructions. Not hearing what has been said can be mistaken for not doing what he is told.
- **Epileptic seizures:** can cause a child to become drowsy and affect their attention span, as well as lead to unusual behaviour.
- **Tourette's syndrome:** involves repetitive, involuntary jerking movements of the body and sudden outbursts of noise or swearing.
- **Attention deficit hyperactivity disorder (ADHD):** this is more than just hyperactive behaviour and leads to lack of concentration and disruptive behaviour. The symptoms can include poor attention, hyperactivity, clumsiness, aggression, low self-esteem.

If you think there may be underlying medical problems, always check with your health visitor or GP as soon as possible. Talk to nursery or school – they can help you spot abnormal behaviour and, where necessary, refer you to a specialist.

Much of this chapter has been good old common-sense, but often common-sense is what parents forget when their toddler is dismantling the house or their four-year-old has just bitten his baby brother. Taking a no-nonsense approach, however, will prepare your child for when it is time to move on from home to other childcare, nursery or school.

CHAPTER 9
nanny's childcare choices

If you plan to return to work after the birth of your child, your first big decision will be who to trust to look after your little one. You have a number of choices, depending on your situation and budget. There are nannies, childminders, au pairs and nurseries, or for the very fortunate, a willing and young-at-heart granny living nearby. How, though, do you pick what's right for *your* child? Nanny can only advise on childcare, as she knows that every family is unique and what works for your sister or friend may not work for you. This chapter therefore gives you the information you need to make the best decision for *your* family.

Planning Ahead

When it comes to planning childcare, two words are invaluable: think ahead. Childcare facilities get booked up months in advance, especially in cities, so it's best to check out your options before your child is born. Nanny knows of super-organised parents who put their child's name down for a place at their preferred nursery after their first scan. Make sure you plan early, do your research and make provisional decisions before the birth while you are still getting a night's sleep. Here's what Nanny recommends when planning childcare:

Nanny's Childcare Checklist:
- Plan ahead – find out what is available in your area.
- Keep it simple – try and get something as close as possible to home or your workplace.
- Childcare is expensive so budget for it.
- Ask your employer for flexible working hours.

Flexibility is the key if you are returning to work. Always have a chat with your employer or HR advisor before your return (better still, before you go on maternity leave) about working flexible hours. Find out, too, if you can work from home when your child is sick. Some mums find it is easier going back to work part-time as this gives them the best of both worlds. Remember to look at all options for childcare facilities while you can, just in case you change your mind once junior arrives.

Childcare in your Home

You have a number of options for childcare at home. Whether you want a nanny, an au pair or a babysitter, Nanny can advise you what to look for.

CHOOSING A NANNY

Nannies look after your children in the environment they know best – your home. A nanny will do the school run, prepare meals and, if it is in her contract, undertake some household duties. Having a nanny, if you can afford it, means that the family routine remains the same. Additionally, if you are running late from work, a nanny will often be able to stay until you arrive. A huge bonus for working parents is that there will be no exhausting school runs during rush hour and you still have control over routine, diet and daytime activities. However, you *must* have the right nanny for you. She may be living in your home, and parents often have difficulty adjusting to life with a nanny.

If you do employ a nanny, you will need to negotiate terms and conditions before she starts work. To avoid any misunderstandings you need to set out what you expect from her – and what she expects from you. You will need to ask the following questions:

Nanny's Nanny Checklist – What You Expect from Her:
- Be clear about her duties. Is she responsible solely for childcare or do you want her to carry out other nursery duties as well, such as the child's cleaning and laundry? Would you like her to do general family housework on top? If so, expect her to negotiate more pay.
- Tell her the hours you need her to work and the salary she will receive (make it clear if this is net or gross).
- Be clear about whether you want her to live in or out.
- If you are not providing her with transport, you need to ensure she has her own car. Check her insurance as she needs appropriate cover to carry children as part of her job. Make sure her car is roadworthy.
- Ensure she has up-to-date CRB (Criminal Records Bureau) clearance or an equivalent certificate.
- Ensure she has an up-to-date first aid certificate.

What Your Nanny Expects from You:
- If she will be using her own car, how will you reimburse her for petrol and other vehicle expenses?
- If she will be living in, what is her accommodation and will she have her own bathroom?
- Will she accompany the family on holiday? If so, what will be paid for and what will her hours be?
- How much annual leave will she get? Ensure you provide the legal minimum or more.

Remember as her employer, you will be responsible for National Insurance and tax. Always check with the agency about any additional payments, such as a pension, that your nanny might be entitled to.

NANNY'S TOP TIP

Always accompany the prospective nanny on a short drive to ensure you are satisfied with her driving before appointing her.

Make sure everything is clear right from the start and recorded in the contract. Don't forget to state your house rules on those small personal details that could become irritating, such as whether smoking is permitted or boyfriends are allowed to stay over. If you have chosen your nanny through an agency, they will help to iron out any difficulties before contracts are signed. Once the nanny is in employment, the agency may continue to assist in resolving any problems. Allow a probationary period of a month, as this gives both nanny and family the option to bail out if there is a clash of character or other issues.

If you do choose a nanny to look after your children, the most important requirement for you, as parents – and one that is most often forgotten – is to ask yourselves whether the nanny has the right personality for your family and does she seem genuinely to like your children. Nanny recommends a trial weekend at home together before anyone signs a contract.

Sometimes parents 'presume' that the nanny should be doing things, so it is vital that you set monthly or weekly meetings, or have informal chats, to make sure all is running smoothly. It is very common to hear criticisms of nannies from the mother. This is often because she feels guilty and undermined as the nanny is taking away some of her role as a parent. Check your behaviour: are you being critical of her work because of your own insecurity or because she is failing in her duties? Also, if she is living in, make it clear that you and your partner need time together. Many complaints from parents are often about nannies being there when they need quiet time with their 'significant other'.

There are other nanny options. Many families choose to have a maternity nurse during the first few weeks at home with their new baby. Maternity nurses are nannies who have received additional training in the care of newborns. Most nanny agencies will be able to recommend maternity nurses in your area (see Chapter 1 for more details).

Another way to make nannies affordable is to opt for a nanny share. This means two things: one family employs a nanny but she looks after children from two families and they share the costs, or the nanny works part-time for two families (for example, two and a half days per family). Obviously, this makes having a nanny much cheaper. You can often find information about nanny sharing through the internet, nanny agencies or local advertisements.

CHOOSING AN AU PAIR

An au pair from another country can be a cheaper option to help at home with the children. You get some assistance with childcare in return for food, lodging and help with the English language. There are a number of au pair agencies in the UK. However, you must realise, right from the start, that an au pair is untrained and often very young. It is best not to look at an au pair as a child carer, but as someone who will help you collect the children from school and keep an eye on them at home.

The same rules apply as for choosing a nanny: pick an au pair who loves being with children and has the right personality for your family. Remember an au pair is far from home and living with a new family, so there might be boyfriend problems, tantrums and tearful phone calls home. Some parents feel that having an au pair can be as stressful as having another child in the house. However, if you get a good au pair, it can be a fabulous way of introducing your children to another language and culture, and can take the pressure off you too.

CHOOSING A BABYSITTER

Everyone uses a babysitter at some time or another. Essentially they are part of your at-home childcare arrangements too. The best babysitters are people you know or trust – or people who are recommended. A few ground rules always help when picking a new babysitter:

Nanny's Babysitter Rules:
- No smoking or alcohol while the children are in their care.
- No friends or boyfriends allowed in the house without your permission.
- The babysitter must check on the children regularly during the session. Nanny recommends every 15 minutes for small babies, even if you have a baby listen-in device.
- Make sure they have your phone numbers and those of a neighbour or relative in case of an emergency.
- Ensure she knows your home address in case she needs to call an ambulance.

HOUSE HUSBANDS AND STAY-AT-HOME MUMS

Many families decide that one parent does not return to work. If you choose to be a 'stay-at-home mum' or 'house husband', make sure your child has an opportunity to meet other children. There are many activities you can take part in: join a playgroup, meet up

NANNY'S TOP TIP

For a younger baby, put him to bed and kiss him goodnight before your babysitter arrives and you get ready to go out. Seeing mummy looming over his cot looking different, with her hair up and wearing earrings and make-up, may make your child cry and leave him unsettled for the evening.

with some other parents to go to the park, or enrol in a baby swimming or music group.

All full-time carers need a break at some point, so make sure there is one thing that you can look forward to for yourself. If you haven't got a relative or friend who can help out, take a walk with the pram so that your baby falls asleep and plan to end your trip at a café sitting with a coffee and a newspaper and a sleeping baby (hopefully).

GRANNY NANNY

If you have relatives who live locally who can help with childcare, perhaps granny, you are very lucky. You will have none of the worries of settling in your child, as granny is already part of your child's life, and this home-grown childcare will probably cost you nothing. The most reassuring thing for any parent is when they know their children are being looked after by someone who loves them as much as they do.

Many grandparents take on childcare responsibilities but it can be hard work – looking after a busy toddler can be tiring even for a 30-year-old; when you are over 60 it can be exhausting. Also, granny and grandpa may have different ideas of bringing up children than you do – and unlike nannies or childminders who are paid to listen to your views, granny may choose to ignore them.

Nanny therefore advises not to overstretch grandparents and always have other childcare options readily available.

Childcare away from Home

The options for childcare away from the family home include childminders and nurseries. As your child will be spending much of his day away from you, it may take more time for him to settle in.

CHOOSING A CHILDMINDER

A registered childminder can care for up to three children in her own home; how many children she cares for at any one time depends on their ages. Childminders in most countries are required by law to have some sort of criminal records check (in the UK this is a CRB clearance) and to be registered with, and inspected by, a local governing body. They usually have a basic childcare qualification and first aid training.

If you are working full-time, your child will be spending much of his time with the childminder, so be prepared for your little one to run to her for a cuddle and not mummy, who has just arrived at the door from work. This is very common, so make sure you are emotionally prepared to take second place – bursting into tears because your baby appears to like the childminder better will not help.

There are many advantages to leaving your child with a minder: they are generally parents themselves; your child will be cared for in a home environment and you will have a degree of flexibility on hours. You can find out what childminders are working in your area by contacting the local council or national childminding associations. Once you have a shortlist of candidates, your next step is to find out what availability they have and visit while she has children there.

Nanny's Childminder Checklist:
- Does she make you and your child welcome?
- Is she interested in your child?
- Do you like the other children?
- Observe how she talks and plays with them.
- Check the rooms and the outdoor play space.
- Find out what food she will cook.
- What are the kitchen facilities like?
- What is the notice period if your situation changes?

Another important factor, which many parents forget, is to ascertain whether you have the same approach to good and bad behaviour. It's no good you having strict rules preventing your child jumping up and down on the furniture at home and crayoning on the walls if he is going to be allowed to do this at the childminder's, or vice versa. Make sure, then, that you are both consistent with how you will manage your child's behaviour.

Finally, most childminders tick all the right boxes – otherwise they could not be registered. Most of them will have a good indoor and outdoor play space, pictures on the walls and healthy food. However, it all comes down to whether you feel the atmosphere and her personality are right for your child, so Nanny suggests you rely on your instincts as a parent. Your decision on whether the childminder is right for your child is, once again, down to your own personal feelings and observations, as well as recommendations from parents you know and trust.

CHOOSING A NURSERY OR CRÈCHE

There are nurseries in almost every village, town and city. They can be council-run, private or affiliated to a local school. Many parents prefer the nursery environment because it prepares their children for the routine of 'big' school and they spend their days with other children of the same age. Nurseries are often a good option for busy parents because they remain open all year round. A team of nursery staff can also be a bonus as they can provide a range of structured activities appropriate to the age of the children. Also, unlike nannies and childminders, if a member of staff is sick there are enough people to provide cover.

For all parents considering a nursery, it is important to visit early to meet the staff and get a feel for the place. It is also good to talk to other parents; there will be a range of opinions but it's worth getting a straw poll on which ones local parents think are best. Your first visit will be better without your child, but once you have made a decision, take your child along with you.

Nanny's Nursery Checklist:
- Is there a warm welcome from the staff?
- Does it have a calm, bright, friendly and stimulating environment?
- Are the children happy and safe?
- Is there an outside play area?
- Is the food healthy and freshly cooked?
- Does the nursery supply milk and nappies for small babies?
- Will they take monthly payment or do they expect you to pay by the term?
- What is the minimum number of days per week you can book?
- Do they cover 52 weeks per year or follow school holidays? (Nurseries attached to a school generally keep to term times.)
- If closed during school holidays, do they offer other holiday options?

All nurseries are highly regulated and will probably provide everything on this checklist. They all set out to attract parents – after all, they are the ones who will be paying the fees – so what you need to know is how to look for the small things that make a nursery *exceptional*. This is information that only Nanny knows.

Nanny's Perfect Nursery Checklist:
- A nursery following the Norland approach sets out to replicate family life by ensuring that the children are supervised in mixed age groups (although there are separate areas for young babies to sleep).
- When you walk around the nursery, look at it from the point of view of a child. If you were one, two or three, what would you see? Pictures should be at child level and inspire and encourage the children. Parents love to see pictures by the children, but the best nurseries have a mix of children's paintings and others of famous art, nature and landscapes.
- A good nursery encourages a love of music – from classical to jazz. The children should have music to listen to and musical instruments to play along with.
- Check if the nursery uses television to entertain the children. Nanny would never choose a nursery which uses television at all.
- Good nurseries have indoor and outdoor play areas and the children decide when and where to play throughout the day. Waterproofs and wellies are available so that they can go out in all weathers and experience the elements.
- Meals are healthy and include fresh fruit and vegetables, not cooked in microwaves.

Nanny would look for all of these things in a nursery. The reason why they are important is that they encourage important social and emotional skills: independence; the ability to concentrate, to sit still and listen; the ability to recognise the needs of others; and self-responsibility. These are the essential skills every child needs before he enters mainstream education, but they are also things that will help him to grow up a happy and well-balanced child.

Childcare Back-up

Whatever you choose, be it a nanny, registered childminder or the local nursery, always have childcare back-up. If you or your child are ill and cannot get to nursery, or the childminder or nanny is sick, you will need someone else to help look after your child. When you are selecting a childminder, it is worth finding out what measures are in place if she is ill. If your childminder or nanny rings you at work to say she is sick, you will need an instant alternative if you cannot down tools and rush home.

Many childcare professionals have a back-up in place, but always check for yourself. This works both ways, as when your child is ill, you will have to take time off work, as the childminder or nursery will not take a sick child. All nurseries have strict rules on illness, so be prepared for the fact that should your child have diarrhoea, a rash, cold or flu symptoms, or conjunctivitis, they will not be allowed to attend. Some parents keep some leave aside to cover for emergencies, or make sure there is a relative or friend who can provide back-up.

It is worth bearing in mind that you may make your childcare choice and later discover that it is not working for you or your child. When making your decision, trust your instincts as a parent and your intimate knowledge of your child's personality. If you have looked at all the options available, you will be well prepared if you do need to change. It's always worth having a 'Plan B'. However, Nanny's advice here is don't take your child away at the first sign of a problem. Remember, it will take time for him to settle into any new childcare routine.

Prepare Yourself and Your Child

Many mothers feel guilty when they finally leave their child with the childminder/au pair/nanny/nursery. You may not be prepared for your reaction. Guilt goes hand in hand with being a working parent, and it is not helped by the coverage from some of the media. For many mothers, the worst part is feeling that they are leaving their child with someone they don't know – someone who is not 'Mum'. Based on years of experience, however, Nanny can reassure you that most children settle in to their new routine eventually.

GETTING YOUR CHILD READY FOR THE BIG DAY

Once you have made the decision on who will be looking after your child, it's good to prepare him for the change in his routine. How he responds will depend on his character. Some children will find the transition to childcare difficult, while others will take this new experience in their stride. Whatever the character of your child, you need to help him prepare for this big change – and when you are under five years old, it is a *big* change.

Ensure your child is feeling happy and secure, and help him feel confident about his new routine. There are many tricks of the trade to make your child's transition to childcare run as smoothly as possible.

Nanny's First Day Checklist:
- Find some story books about starting at nursery – check out the local library.
- Explain what nursery or playgroup is like. He will have new friends and new toys, and it will be great fun, but do it casually. If you overdo it, it may not live up to his expectations.
- Visit the childminder or nursery with your child well

in advance. It may take some settling in to ensure a happy child.

- Arrange to meet up with another parent and child from the group before going; your child will then have a friend when he arrives.

When the big day arrives and you drop your child at the childminder's or nursery or leave him with nanny, you need to have prepared yourself as well. What would you do if you saw your own mother in floods of tears? You would probably cry too. All mums who are likely to cry must therefore practise before the big day and control their tears. You can cry when you get back in the car, on a friend's shoulder or down the phone to your mum, but don't do it in front of the children. This is a very important day so try to remain calm and breezy. Arrive, introduce yourself, say goodbye and reassure your child that you will be back on time at the end of the day or session, and then leave. If he cries you must not turn back; the likelihood is that he will stop as soon as you are out of sight. If you promise to call to see if he has calmed down, make sure you do so, but don't talk to him directly on the phone. Instead, ask the nursery staff to ensure he knows mummy did ring.

GETTING INTO A ROUTINE

Nanny advises you to get a routine in place at home too – the dash out of the door does not need to be hectic. Encourage older children to take responsibility for their own satchels. By the time he is at school, a child's week can be awfully busy: sports kit on Monday, violin on Tuesday, swimming kit on Wednesday and so on for the next 14 or so years. One of the best ways to stay organised is to draw up a chart or plan with your week plotted out. Nanny recommends using a piece of A3 card, showing days of the week along the top and times down the side. This is essential for a big family, but useful for smaller ones too, as it ensures that everyone is out of the house on time and with the right kit. You can make this even more visually exciting by getting your children to create the artwork with you. With younger children you can use cut-out pictures of musical instruments or swimmers stuck on thin card, which can then be placed on the chart with Blu Tac. Encourage reading by giving older children a word written out on a piece of card – 'spelling book', 'violin', 'sports kit' and so on.

The best place to put the chart is on the inside of the front or back door, then everyone can check as they leave that they have everything they need for the day. Encouraging the children to check the schedule helps you, but also allows them to develop a sense of responsibility. Ask the children to check twice: on the morning as they leave but also the night before, so that all relevant bags can be placed out ready. This will help avoid a mad panic on a school morning as you remember that the sports kit is still wet and muddy in the washing basket, and you left the violin at grandma's. With Nanny's sound advice, by the time all your children are in mainstream education, your morning routine should be calm, organised and a breeze … on most days!

nanny's
last word

At some point, all children grow up and Nanny isn't needed any more. However, unlike Mary Poppins or Nanny McPhee, *Nanny in a Book* will be a permanent member of your family, even if she's sitting on the bookshelf, well thumbed and much loved. Rest assured, she'll be there for when the children she has helped raise have children themselves, because when it comes to childcare her common-sense advice is timeless ...

the norland way

In 1892, Norland College's founder, Emily Ward, was the first to recognise that the best nursery nurses needed proper training. However, defining the 'Norland way' is as difficult as carrying a baby in one arm and a laundry basket in the other while reading to a toddler because Norland Nannies constantly change with the times. They are at the cutting edge of childcare. Being the leading light in childcare, though, does not mean that Norland has lost any of its tradition or the sound advice that gave birth to the phrase 'Nanny knows best'. Today, Nanny knows an awful lot, and she is on hand to advise and support any family or childcare setting in which she works, bringing Norland's unique way with children to everyone she meets.

The Norland Code of Professional Responsibilities is adhered to by all Norland Nannies. If anyone is found to be in breach of the Code, they may be struck off Norland's employment register. So, what makes a Norland Nanny so special?

- **She allows childhood to last.**
- **She values the individual child, letting them learn and grow.**
- **Care is centred on the child.**
- **She never shouts, never smacks, never does physical or emotional harm.**
- **She always smiles, remains calm, nurtures and loves.**
- **She is organised and super efficient but flexible.**
- **She never calls a child 'kid' as it shows a lack of respect.**

- She is authoritative, not authoritarian.
- She knows that 'love never fails'.

If love and respect are the basis for your family life, then you are halfway there. If the rest of Norland's knowledge can be passed on to you, your own children and your children's children, then this book has truly served its purpose. And when the wind changes, Nanny can depart knowing that her work is done.

ACKNOWLEDGEMENTS

Many thanks to our patient agent Lyndsey Posner, to the Norland Nannies who have given their advice, and to our boys.

INDEX